NEW ZEA LAND

Travel with Marco Polo Insider Tips

INSIDER TIP
Your shortcut to a great experience

MARCO POLO
TOP HIGHLIGHTS

HAURAKI GULF ⭐ 1
Golden sandy beaches and turquoise seas: cast off for Waiheke or Great Barrier Island and you'll feel a world away from Auckland.

➤ p. 56, North Island

NINETY MILE BEACH ⭐ 2
An endless surfing beach that stretches 55 miles (not 90!) from Ahipara to Scott Point in Northland. The sun sinks bright red into the sea in the evenings.

➤ p. 50, North Island

COROMANDEL PENINSULA ⭐ 3
This peninsula is perfect for beach-hopping, kayaking and surfing (photo).
📷 *Tip: Walk from Hahei along the coastal path to Cathedral Cove and take a photo of the beach framed by the rock walls of the cave. For the best pictures, make sure you visit at low tide.*

➤ p. 57, North Island

TONGARIRO ALPINE CROSSING ⭐ 4
Smouldering craters and black lava rocks make for one the best day tours in the world.
📷 *Tip: Visit the Emerald Lakes – three crater lakes of emerald-green water at an altitude of 1700m. Try a bird's eye view for a particularly impressive shot.*

➤ p. 71, North Island

TE PAPA TONGAREWA ⭐ 5
Earthquakes included! You just can't get enough at the interactive Museum of New Zealand.

➤ p. 81, North Island

CATLINS ⭐ 6

Sea lions and penguins dominate the beaches here in the wild southwest.

📷 *Tip: Take a photo of the lighthouse at Nugget Point from the shore path in the evening.*

➤ p. 106, South Island

GLACIERS IN THE RAINFOREST ⭐ 7

The Franz Josef Glacier and the smaller Fox Glacier emerge from lush vegetation.

➤ p. 122 and p. 124, South Island

ABEL TASMAN NATIONAL PARK ⭐ 8

On foot or by kayak: discover New Zealand's smallest, but by no means less beautiful, national park.

➤ p. 131, South Island

STEWART ISLAND ⭐ 9

Watch kiwis scurry through untouched nature as you approach the "end of the world".

📷 *Tip: Capture the blood-red sunrise on the island of "glowing skies" in Halfmoon Bay.*

➤ p. 106, South Island

MILFORD SOUND ⭐ 10

The majestic Mitre Peak towers more than 1500m into the sky on the shore of the fjord.

📷 *Tip: Head to the pier early in the morning before the tourists arrive and as the first rays of sunlight break through the clouds at Mitre Peak.*

➤ p. 112, South Island

CONTENTS

NORTH ISLAND

SOUTH ISLAND

CONTENTS

☉	Plan your visit	🍴	Eating/drinking	👕	Rainy day activities
$ – $$$	Price categories	🛍	Shopping	🐗	Budget activities
(*)	Premium-rate phone number	🍸	Going out	😎	Family activities
		🏖	Top beaches	🚩	Classic experiences

(📖 A2) Refers to the removable pull-out map
(0) Located off the map

Mangamaunu beach, near Kaikoura

BEST OF NEW ZEALAND

Mount Taranaki: the peak of the moody mountain is often hidden by cloud

BEST ☂

WHEN IT RAINS

ACTIVITIES TO BRIGHTEN YOUR DAY

DELVE INTO THE UNDERWORLD
In the *Waitomo Glowworm Caves* (photo) the green twinkling of thousands of glow-worms glimmers in the darkness. Glide by boat through the grotto or go caving on a *Lost World Tour* deep underground.
➤ p. 67, North Island

FANTASY FOR REAL
Tour the Oscar-winning *Weta Workshop Studios* in Wellington to see how *The Hobbit* or *The Lord of the Rings* achieved enhanced reality with special effects.
➤ p. 83, North Island

A DAY AT THE SOUTH POLE
In the *International Antarctic Centre* on the outskirts of Christchurch you can withstand an indoor snowstorm, watch penguins waddle through the snow or travel to the south pole in the 3-D cinema.
➤ p. 95, South Island

GLIMPSE OF THE PAST
How tough was life for New Zealand's first settlers? The *Toitu Otago Settlers Museum* in Dunedin offers some answers – here, the first gold diggers and sheep stockmen stare at you from among hundreds of old paintings.
➤ p. 101, South Island

HISTORIC CINEMA
There are cinemas in New Zealand that date from the time when people said, "We're going to the pictures". Visit an art deco palace from the 1930s with red cushioned seats and film-ready façades, such as the *Rialto* in Dunedin or the *Regent* in Hokitika.
➤ p. 103 and p. 126, South Island

MOUNTAIN SPA
On rainy days, you can enjoy the warm bubbling mountain water of Queenstown's *Onsen Hot Pools* on the rocky cliffs above Shotover River.
➤ p. 117, South Island

BEST 🐷
ON A BUDGET

FOR SMALLER WALLETS

CINEMA ON THE BEACH

On *Takapuna Movie Nights*, in January and February, films are shown free of charge on the white sandy beach of Takapuna, a neighbourhood in the north of Auckland.

➤ p. 55, North Island

MULTIFACETED AOTEAROA

At Wellington's *Te Papa Tongarewa* (photo) you can discover what New Zealand is all about. Admission to the Kiwis' national museum is free and its fabulous interactive experiences – e.g. a simulated earthquake – are popular.

➤ p. 81, North Island

DEMOCRACY LIVE

Women's suffrage since 1893 and a female Prime Minister who had a baby while in office: find out more about New Zealand's progressive democracy during a free guided tour through the *Parliament Buildings* in Wellington.

➤ p. 82, North Island

BOTANY FOR FREE

The perfect spot to learn about Aotearoa's flora. Admission is free at the *New Zealand Gardens* in Christchurch's *Botanic Gardens*.

➤ p. 94, South Island

CREATIVE MICROCOSM

The *Dog with Two Tails* is a café-bar in Dunedin where new bands regularly appear for free. Whether surf pop or jazz is your thing, they have it here. Top entertainment for the price of a beer!

➤ p. 103, South Island

DIVE WITH DOLPHINS

Would you prefer not to spend money on an expensive boat tour and yet want to see dolphins while swimming? Then head for *Porpoise Bay* in the Catlins. Here, there are plenty of curious Hector's dolphins that will dive through the surf with you.

➤ p. 106, South Island

BEST

WITH CHILDREN

DUNE SURFING

The perfect picture for the photo album: when the entire family plunges together on body boards down the 100-m-high dunes of the dune landscape in *Te Paki* on Cape Reinga (photo).
➤ p.50, North Island

STAY DRY UNDER THE SEA

What's lurking in the Pacific? At *Kelly Tarlton's Sealife Aquarium*, plexiglass tunnels lead through aquariums with 1,500 sea creatures, including sharks and turtles. In the Antarctic section, penguins from the South Pole even waddle through the snow.
➤ p. 54, North Island

FOLLOW THE CHEEPS

Kiwis are rarely seen in the wild, but you'll be able to see these timid birds at the *Kiwi House* in the small town of Otorohanga. Everything there focuses on their survival, so kiwi chicks are not a rare sight.
➤ p.68, North Island

ORIGINAL ACCOMMODATION

Give your kids something to remember, and stay somewhere totally original. Spend the night in *Woodlyn Park* near the Waitomo Glowworm Caves where you can sleep in an old steamer moored on dry land. Or there's the cave dwelling, just like the one from *The Hobbit*.
➤ p. 68, North Island

POTTY MOUTH

Kids can play for hours at the *Margaret Mahy Playground* in Christchurch. With trampolining, ziplining or hopping in the fountains, it's the biggest playground in the southern hemisphere. There are even talking toilets!
➤ p.96, South Island

BEST

CLASSIC EXPERIENCES

ONLY IN NEW ZEALAND

KAURI GOD

There are hardly any old buildings in New Zealand, but you can see the world's oldest kauri tree. *Tane Mahuta*, the 51-m giant "God of the Forest" in *Waipoua Kauri Forest*, is estimated to be 2,000 years old. Incredible!

➤ p. 49, North Island

WARRIOR DANCES

Before every game, the New Zealand rugby team challenges the opposing team with a battle dance (photo). The *Haka* is an old Maori tradition – a ceremonial dance performed country-wide in schools and sports clubs. Would you like to try? At the *Haka shows* in Rotorua spectators are allowed on the stage.

➤ p. 62, North Island

A WORLD BEFORE OUR TIME

Stroll through forests full of rare parrots in Wellington's *Zealandia*, one of the world's few eco-sanctuaries in the heart of a city, and get a feeling of how things may have looked in New Zealand long before our time.

➤ p. 82, North Island

COUNT KIWIS

These flightless, hen-shaped birds with long beaks are native to New Zealand. Sadly, predators imported from Europe like rats and cats have almost wiped them out. However, around 20,000 kiwis still live in the *Rakiura National Park* on *Stewart Island*, so you'll have a good chance of seeing one there.

➤ p. 107, South Island

SOUTHERN GLOW

Aurora Australis is the name given to the spectacular light show in the southern hemisphere sky that you can see, if you're lucky, on *Stewart Island*.

➤ p. 107, South Island

GET TO KNOW NEW ZEALAND

It's not just a cliche to say that New Zealand has a lot of sheep

DISCOVER NEW ZEALAND

Civil servants busy themselves in the "Beehive" next to Wellington's Parliament Buildings

At the tip of the green fern's frond, the sunshine is reflected in the dew, while waves break on the white sandy beach behind. Screeching seabirds hunt fish in the blue sea. Rainforest surrounds the long glaciers; deep fjords and lakes reflect snow-covered mountain peaks, and volcanoes soar into the steel-blue sky. In some places, nature's forces even break through the Earth's surface.

SOMETHING DIFFERENT AROUND EVERY CORNER

New Zealand is as varied as a pocket-sized version of Europe. Its area is about 24,000km² larger than the United Kingdom, but its population of approximately 5.1 million is not even a tenth of that of the UK.

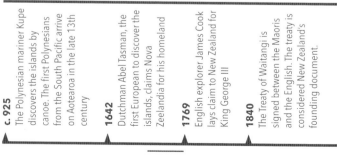

c. 925
The Polynesian mariner Kupe discovers the islands by canoe. The first Polynesians from the South Pacific arrive on Aotearoa in the late 13th century

1642
Dutchman Abel Tasman, the first European to discover the islands, claims Nova Zeelandia for his homeland

1769
English explorer James Cook lays claim to New Zealand for King George III

1840
The Treaty of Waitangi is signed between the Maoris and the English. The treaty is considered New Zealand's founding document.

SET YOUR SIGHTS ON PARADISE

Admittedly, it's not exactly round the corner. When you're finally here, you will need time to relax and unwind. But anyone who has travelled on two long-haul flights, each about 11 hours, and has overcome the jetlag, will find a fabulous and varied travel destination. It has an excellent network of tourist accommodation, easy transport and plenty of attractions for the several million people who visit each year. The country at the bottom of the world is no longer an insider's tip – sorry! But it's still breathtakingly beautiful, even if the main attractions in New Zealand's high summer season from December to February are jam-packed.

A DREAM FOR OUTDOOR SPORTS

No matter whether it's with hiking boots, in fins or snowboard boots – active holidaymakers can enjoy a great adventure here. You can hike across the entire country on the new Te Araroa Walkway or tour by bike on the Great Cycle Track – from Cape Reinga in the north as far as Bluff in the extreme south. The national parks include nine Great Walks as well as numerous shorter trails and many other natural wonders. New Zealanders often enjoy exploring nature too – "going bush" is not only a popular pastime for tourists. If you want more excitement, you can leap (with a harness!) off bridges, out of a plane or from a cliff – and expect impressive views. The climate is moderate and European, and the Kiwis – as the locals call themselves – are very friendly.

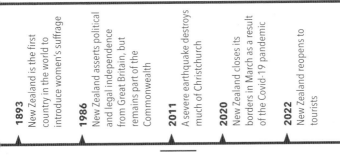

1893
New Zealand is the first country in the world to introduce women's suffrage

1986
New Zealand asserts political and legal independence from Great Britain, but remains part of the Commonwealth

2011
A severe earthquake destroys much of Christchurch

2020
New Zealand closes its borders in March as a result of the Covid-19 pandemic

2022
New Zealand reopens to tourists

STARRING MOUNTAINS, LAKES, BEACHES & VOLCANOES

Everything is easy to discover here: the Pacific Ocean in the east, the Tasman Sea in the west and, in between, North and South Island as well as hundreds of smaller islands dotted in the sea around them. In the partly subtropical north, there are excursions to the rainforests, beaches and lakes, volcanoes and green mountains to keep you busy. On South Island, things are more primal, with alpine mountains, glaciers and fjords and an unfathomably vast hiking and mountaineering paradise. The Fiordland National Park is one of the country's three UNESCO World Natural Heritage Sites.

THE SEA IS NEVER FAR

And then the coastline, all 15,000km of it. In New Zealand, you will never be more than 120km from the sea. So, if you hanker after salty air, it'll be no more than a few hours before you can brave the waves on a surfboard, kayak or stand-up paddle board. You can also find city life on the coast, although this is restricted to Auckland, which is the biggest city in the north of North Island, and the capital city Wellington on the southern tip. Christchurch and Dunedin in the south are fairly small. Incidentally, make sure you leave all the beautiful shells on the beach! The 44 marine reserves are all "no take" zones, meaning you are not allowed to remove anything from here.

UNIQUE FOUR-LEGGED FRIENDS (MOSTLY!)

New Zealand's animals are legendary. There are birds that prefer to walk rather than fly (and that's not just the kiwi). Rare dolphins play with surfers in the waves; around the islands there are numerous whales, seals and seabird species. Anything dangerous? Other than sharks, absolutely not! In New Zealand, unlike its Australian neighbour, you can expect many unique species that are usually perfectly harmless and look genuinely cute. Okay, except perhaps for the scary weta, a fat giant grasshopper, which might drop on your shoulder in caves. But it's harmless too.

YOUNG EARTH

New Zealand is a geological newbie, one of the newest countries on the planet. It only separated 80–100 million years ago from the super-continent Gondwana. Thanks to its youth, the country has one of the world's most active volcanic fields. It rattles and rumbles in different corners, and mini earthquakes are the norm. The thermal regions around Rotorua on North Island will certainly take your breath away – and that's not only down to their powerful stench.

EXPERIENCE MAORI CULTURE

If you are interested, you can gain a deep insight into the culture of the Maori. At Maori ceremonial sites, the Maraeas, you can see for yourself the famous Haka,

AT A GLANCE

5,100,000
inhabitants

Greater London: 8,908,000

15,134km
coastline

UK: 12,429km

268,021km²
area

UK: 243,610km²

TALLEST MOUNTAIN: MOUNT COOK

3,755m

Ben Nevis: 1,345m

THE WORLD'S STEEPEST ROAD: BALDWIN STREET, DUNEDIN

35%
GRADIENT

MOST RAINY DAYS IN A YEAR: MILFORD SOUND

200

430 BUNGY JUMPS IN 24 HOURS
put New Zealander Mike Heard into the *Guinness World Records*

AUCKLAND

is the largest city with 1.7 million inhabitants; every third New Zealander lives there

BIGGEST SPORTING STARS
The All Blacks rugby team have a 78% win rate

SHEEP ON SOUTH ISLAND:
15.4 MILLION
PEOPLE: 1.5 MILLION

or warrior dance. According to Maori tradition, the wife of Kupe, the legendary Polynesian mariner, was said to have been the first to discover New Zealand and named the islands "Aotearoa" – land of the long white cloud – the Maori name for their homeland. The first settlers with their canoes arrived from the South Pacific in the 13th century; nowadays, the proud culture of the Maori, whose population is estimated as 735,000, enjoys a comparatively high status in the country. The 1840 Treaty of Waitangi established sovereignty of the British Crown and the indigenous population.

NOT A DESTINATION IF YOU'RE ON A BUDGET

Europeans first arrived at the green, fertile paradise in the 18th century and immediately recognised its economic benefit. The consequence: military conflicts and, until today, disputed territorial claims. In a country that offers abundant space, land ownership has traditionally been a point of contention. In Auckland, land and real estate prices are among the highest in the world. And in general the cost of living is very high: New Zealand is not a budget destination. Many things have to be transported from far across the world. Even the cost of local products is often higher – don't be surprised if a bottle of Sauvignon Blanc from Marlborough is more expensive than it would be back home. The Kiwis love drinking wine or beer. They often can't afford many other treats. With an average income of about NZ$58,000 (approx. US$36,000/£30,000), many people have high debts and often need a second job to make ends meet.

A CLEAR COURSE THROUGH THE PANDEMIC

Politically, New Zealand is still a member of the Commonwealth, the King is the representative head of state. However, the country is governed independently of the Crown and many people demand full independence from Great Britain. During the 2017 parliamentary elections, there was a major political change when the then 37-year-old Labour party leader, Jacinda Ardern, replaced Conservative Bill English. In October 2020, Ardern was re-elected for a further three years. New Zealanders widely held her in high regard for her unwavering stance during the Covid-19 pandemic. But she resigned in January 2023 and was succeeded as Labour party leader and prime minister by Chris Hipkins.

STILL WORK TO BE DONE

Despite the Kiwis' love of nature, the image of clean and green New Zealand unfortunately falls into the category of misleading advertising. The New Zealanders are really playing catch-up over environmental protection, especially waste management, the banning of plastic and protecting waterways. However, with almost 90 per cent of the electricity supply from renewable energy, the country is well on its way to breaking renewable electricity records. Hydro- and

The largest immigrant population in New Zealand are sheep, introduced by European settlers

wind power, as well as geothermal heat, are the main energy sources. In fact, New Zealand wants to become carbon neutral by 2050.

DISCOVER A SLOWER PACE

The most important advice for your trip to the bottom of the world: take time to appreciate the country and its people. Slow travel away from the main tourist attractions shows you the real New Zealand. Along bumpy gravel tracks and with the car covered in a thick layer of dust inside and out, you'll find rustic locations, deserted beaches and down-to-earth, uncomplicated, informal locals who love to chat and sometimes invite tourists to the next barbecue. Please bring your own drinks! BYO is also popular in some restaurants. And you can stay casual! Nobody here needs to be too dressed up, not even in the evenings. The standard attire is shorts and sandals for every occasion and season.

ONE STEP CLOSER TO HEAVEN

New Zealand is a holiday destination for active nature lovers. But those who prefer to watch will also feel at home here; the main thing is to be outdoors in the clean, fresh air. There is hardly any air pollution in New Zealand. That makes stargazing an unforgettable experience. So, take a deep breath, then gaze into the sky and count the shooting stars!

UNDERSTAND NEW ZEALAND

ALL BLACK

Rugby is a religion, an institution and a cult – and the players are the All Blacks; New Zealand's national team are absolute stars at home. When it comes to championship titles, the small country towers above the rest of the world. The All Blacks (who dress all in black at international events) have ruined many other teams' dreams of winning titles, surely because they are boosted by the fearsome Haka, the Maori warrior dance, which the team performs before every match.

QUESTION OF HONOUR

While rugby is a cult, down-under sailing is simply a question of honour. It's no surprise, seeing as New Zealand is a country surrounded by oceans and was first discovered by mariners. And Auckland is not called "City of Sails" without reason. The Hauraki Gulf is on the doorstep; it's one of the world's best sailing grounds with optimal training conditions for pros as well as amateur sailors. As recently as 2021, the New Zealand team won the America's Cup once again.

A MOVE TO THE BOTTOM OF THE WORLD

New Zealand has become the dream home for more and more people. Before the Covid-19 pandemic, almost 70,000 new residents were accepted every year, mainly from Asia. In 2020, numbers fell to just 6,600, but they rose again in 2021 to around 37,000 new arrivals. Auckland is bursting at the seams. The biggest city with about a third of the total population accepts most of the new citizens. Most jobs are here, but there is a serious lack of residential space, and many old Aucklanders are leaving for booming cities like Tauranga or Whangarei.

NO SWIMMING!

More than half of New Zealand's lakes and rivers are not suitable for swimming. The main problem is cow manure. The dairy sector is New Zealand's biggest industry, and for decades cattle could wander where they wanted. The result is excessive nitrates in rivers and lakes, which means that more than half of all freshwater fish are threatened with extinction. In addition, the countrywide clearance of ancient forests in the past still has negative repercussions today: during heavy rainfall many sediments are washed away from the unstable soil.

IT'S BUBBLING UNDERGROUND

New Zealand has one of the world's most active volcanic fields, and the country rumbles, spits and bubbles in many places. Mount Tongariro spewed rubble and ashes twice in 2012, and its neighbour Mount Ruapehu erupted in 2007. And in 2019, 22 people died on White Island when Whakaari erupted. In Auckland, people are asking when the next eruption will happen. Scientists expect another

The active volcanoes in Tongariro National Park are best observed from a distance

eruption here – but there is no reason to worry, as that could take another few hundred years.

New earthquakes are registered hourly on *geonet.org.nz*, as the country is not only on the Pacific Ring of Fire, but also on two overlapping tectonic plates. The last major quake was at the end of 2016 in Kaikoura on South Island. Two people were killed, and the town was cut off for a long time from the outside world. Tourists had to be transported on ships and by helicopter – that's some holiday experience. In Christchurch, you can still see the aftermath of the disastrous 2011 earthquake that killed 185 people.

MY COUNTRY, YOUR COUNTRY

New Zealand's founding document is the Treaty of Waitangi. On 6 February 1840, the Governor of New Zealand, William Hobson, and about 50 Maori chiefs signed the document that regulated the country's government by the English crown. The Maoris were promised rights to their land, cultural treasures and protection from the British sovereign government. It sounded wonderful at first, but in reality there were heated conflicts and unlawful compulsory acquisitions from the indigenous population. Another problem: there are various versions of the English translation of Te Reo from Maori. Back then, the

Hongi, the traditional Maori greeting, is respectful and wordless

Maoris knew nothing of the concept of "land ownership". The treaty's interpretation still leads to heated controversies today. Since 1975, the Waitangi Tribunal has attempted to regulate controversial decisions, and the Maoris have been paid compensation sums and state territory has been transferred back into their ownership.

Maori culture is present throughout the country: Maori dances, Maori traditions, like the *hongi* traditional greeting, and the Maori language. In 2018, New Zealand's parliament ruled that, from 2025, all schools must teach the indigenous Maori language in addition to English.

KIWI SOUND CULTURE

There's a thriving independent music scene in New Zealand, and some good bands continue to tour the small clubs. Singer/songwriter Aldous Harding from Christchurch, for example, was discovered busking on the street (her latest album is called *Warm Chris*).

Kiwis also flock to see the seven-piece dub-reggae band Fat Freddy's Drop, who have Polynesian-New Zealand roots and are often programmed at local festivals. *Young Blood* from the electro-indie Auckland band The Naked and Famous is often played in bars and cafés around New Zealand.

The singers Lorde (known for her global hit "Royals") and Ladyhawke ("Paris Is Burning") prove with their innovative electro tracks that tomorrow's sound is also being created on the other side of the world.

WHO OR WHAT IS THE KIWI?

Take care with the word "Kiwi". It's a well-meant nickname for a New Zealander. But it's borrowed from the name of a slightly plump, flightless bird with a long beak – the "kiwi bird". Then, there is also the "kiwi fruit" which originally wasn't quite so "Kiwi"; it actually comes from China and is also known as the Chinese gooseberry.

SOUTH SEA TONES

Auckland is the alternative capital city of Samoa. More Samoans live here than anywhere else; in fact, there are almost three times as many Samoans in Auckland as there are in their native capital Apia. Decades ago, sporty youngsters from Samoa not only came to New Zealand because of their rugby talents, but also because of their labour. Until 1962, the South Sea state was governed by New Zealand, and in the 1950s Aotearoa needed lots of workers. The Samoans mainly settled in the south of Auckland. Today, people from the South Pacific communities still meet in the district of Otara at the Saturday market: as well as Samoans, there are immigrants from Fiji, Tonga and the Cook Islands. Those who want to visit the South Pacific islands will do well to learn some *Talofa*, *Bula* and *Mālō e lelei*.

LUXURY HUTS

Living space was and is in short supply, particularly in Auckland. Kiwis are traditionally proud homeowners. Property prices in the city in recent years have risen to an average value of

TRUE OR FALSE?

DON'T LAY IT ON TOO THICK

People who are arrogant or presumptuous aren't popular in New Zealand. No one enjoys Tall Poppy Syndrome, as this type of person is called. Most Kiwis are modest and tend to play down their successes. Even Sir Edmund Hillary, who was the first person, alongside Tenzing Norgay, to summit Mount Everest, never bragged about his records. He never forgot his origins as a modest beekeeper.

SANDALS FOR THE WIN

Kiwi men have a uniform: shorts and sandals. Handy for a quick detour to the beach. They even walk barefoot through the streets without their *jandals* (flip-flops) to show they're just chilled, casual guys.

FANCY DRESS FESTIVALS

New Zealanders always find a reason to don fancy dress. In Napier, at the Art Deco Weekend in February the whole town dresses up in 1920s style. In Oamaru, "the steampunk capital of the world", men and women in Victorian costume are part of the city scene, and not just during the Steampunk Festival in May. In Russell for the Birdman Festival in July, the locals rush into the water with paper wings and compete in the Drag Race.

New Zealand's iconic silver fern grows to the size of a tree and looks best in natural surroundings

about NZ$1.5 million (approx. £770,000 / US$929,000) for a house. Properties were often bought up by domestic and foreign investors and quickly resold for vast profits. The city also needs more homes to house the more than 50,000 New Zealanders who returned home from abroad during the Covid-19 pandemic. The result? Construction everywhere. Major traffic problems and a lack of infrastructure have been put on the back burner for now.

RARE ANIMAL SPECIES

Rare animal species are not unusual in New Zealand. At the top of the list is a 225 million-year-old lizard-like species of tuatara that only lives in the wild on some of the more remote islands. The rarest bird in New Zealand is not, in fact, the kiwi but the flightless takahe, of which only about 300 remain. You can admire this wonderful blue bird in several conservation areas. However, the superstar among the flightless species is still the kiwi, which is active at night. With its long beak and fluffy plumage, it is the animal emblem for the entire nation. Breeding programmes have boosted numbers to about 68,000. In case you're wondering why the kiwi cannot fly at all, it's because there were no predators in New Zealand until settlers arrived, so it had no need to fly. This made the flightless birds easy prey, and over time they were almost completely wiped out. The Department of Conservation is trying

Maoris call the young, unrolled fronds of a silver fern *koru*. These spirals symbolise new beginnings and energy. About 80 per cent of all ferns, trees and flowering plants in New Zealand are endemic. The App *Flora Finder* will help you to identify them.

TOURISM UNDER COVID

Tourists wherever you look! At least that's how it was at all New Zealand's hotspots before the Covid-19 pandemic. In Queenstown, for example, you'd be hard pushed to get a room during the high season from January to March without booking well in advance. Even multi-day hikes in the national parks like the Great Walks had to be booked months ahead. In 2019, 11 million visitors from all over the world came to New Zealand. But during the pandemic, the country suddenly became a sort of "sleeping beauty" – and Kiwis had all their tourist attractions to themselves. From one day to the next, the jet skis on Queenstown's Shotover River, for example, were carrying only 200 people a day instead of the usual 1,200. All this looks set to change as tourism picks up again.

If you want to avoid the crowds and head into the bush as a *freedom camper* you will still have to stick to the rules: wild camping is only permitted at designated sites, and you should always have a chemical toilet and waste water on board! Since the end of 2021, if you're caught camping without permission, you can expect to pay a penalty of up to NZ$1,000.

to systematically control imported rodents, especially possums, which are trapped and poisoned. They might look cute, but the New Zealanders' motto is: "Only a dead possum is a good possum."

SILVER FERN

It decorates the shirts of Kiwi sports stars and is a wonderful route-marker in the forest: *ponga*, silver fern – the big tree fern – is New Zealand's national plant. The underside of the frond shimmers silver so that it can mark the way at night. The Maoris once used the large fronds as roofing material for their houses or to weave mats. The islands also have more than 200 unique ferns in all sizes. The

EATING
SHOPPING
SPORT

Visit New Zealand in winter for top-notch skiing with a view

EATING & DRINKING

You can recognize New Zealanders abroad by the fact that they have a jar of Vegemite on the shelf (it's a savoury spread similar to Marmite). If you want to experience New Zealand with all the senses, you should taste the brown spread – same goes for pavlova (meringue with kiwi fruit and whipped cream) and, of course, grilled lamb chops.

MORNING RITUALS

New Zealanders start the day with a cup of tea with milk or a flat white (which was invented by a barista from Wellington; the Australians are mistaken when they say that they came up with the idea). Breakfast at cafés in New Zealand can range from porridge with fruit and nuts, eggs benedict with slices of avocado, pancakes with caramelized fruits, or freshly baked scones with dates. Clean eating cafés are also popular – they only use organic products and prefer vegetarian or vegan ingredients (chia seed dessert, etc.). On your travels you will find a fish & chip shop and bakery in every small town. Steak & cheese pies and sausage rolls are commonly sold as snacks between meals.

WINERY SUPERSTARS

On your travels, take note of the many vineyards, historic pubs and stalls along the way. New Zealand's biggest wine-growing area is Marlborough on South Island. The climate is ideal as there is hardly any rain, the nights are cool and the days are full of intense sunshine. This produces especially fruity grapes. Connoisseurs can instantly spot the pure and fresh flavour of New Zealand wines when they try a glass of Sauvignon Blanc, such as *Cloudy Bay*. You will also find excellent wines in the vineyards in Central Otago; the *Pinot Noir* is world

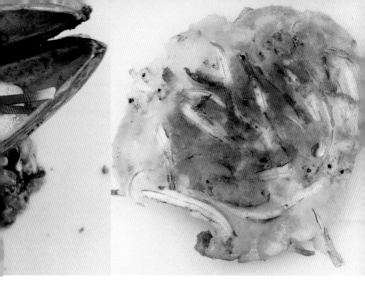

New Zealand specialities include green-lipped mussels (left) and whitebait patties (right)

famous; the vines thrive in the region's rich mineral soil. You can taste plenty of award-winning varieties at *Gibbston Valley* winery. Chardonnay and Syrah are also popular exports from New Zealand. But surprisingly, professional wine cultivation in Aoteaora only began in the 1980s.

AT THE ROADSIDE

The area around Queenstown and Wanaka is well worth visiting for the many fruit orchards. In Cromwell, Central Otago, start with a quick selfie at the giant fruit sculpture made from peaches and pears at the town's entrance before stocking up on fruit. At the Bay of Plenty, roadside stalls sell baskets of avocados at bargain prices. Every region has its own craft beer (e.g. McLeod's from Waipu or Garage Project from Wellington) and celebrates local specialities (oysters from Bluff, langoustines from Kaikoura).

Glass display cases filled with cakes, pies and salads and are also typical in New Zealand cafés. You should definitely try lollie cake, ginger squares or Kumara salad. And don't miss Belgian biscuits (known as "German biscuits" until World War II). They taste of cinnamon and ginger and are covered with a pink sugar glaze.

BARBECUE PROFESSIONALS

In New Zealand you'll constantly hear the phrase, "Shall we have a barbie?", because almost everyone has a gas barbecue in their garden the size of a DJ's mixing desk. Steaks and seafood are grilled on it. Fresh green-lipped mussels – only found in New Zealand – are a favourite. Available at the supermarket, they are the largest mussels in the world and can grow up to 17cm long. In many parks and even in playgrounds there are gas barbecues for public use.

roast lamb, but also typical Kiwi dishes like seafood chowder and steamed green-lipped mussels. However, the culinary habits of the early European settlers are not the only flavours that characterise New Zealand cuisine today, as gourmet influences have arrived from around the world. Sushi (mostly an XXL portion) is available on every corner, and in most fish & chips stores (you should definitely try deep-fried scallops) you will find Chinese food on the menu. In Auckland there are excellent Indian and Asian restaurants.

FROM THE EARTH OVEN

New Zealanders have a relaxed attitude to fine wines

> **INSIDER TIP**
> **Hunt for food in the wilderness**

You can find out about Maori food on outdoor foraging tours, such as the *Kai Waho Experience (kaiwaho.co.nz)* with Maori chef Tom Loughlin at Lake Taupo. Aotoeaora's original settlers had a difficult time finding food. They couldn't hunt land mammals, and had to make do with plants, birds and fish. Their whole existence depended on being able to understand nature. Nowadays, there are descendants of the first Maoris who are happy to show how you catch eels and prepare pikopiko, the rolled-up shoots of the Moku fern. In the geothermal areas of Rotorua, where Maori have lived for centuries, there are plenty of opportunities to sample a specialty from the *hangi* – the traditional Maori earth ovens; sweet potatoes, pork and pumpkin are all wrapped in flax leaves and cooked over hot stones for several hours.

Most cafés close about 5pm. Soon afterwards, from 6pm, the restaurants fill up for dinner (and they often close around 10pm). In so-called BYO restaurants you can bring your own beer and wine.

FUSION CUISINE

Pubs also serve good food. On the menu you'll usually find hearty Old World dishes such as shepherd's pie or

TODAY'S SPECIALS

Apéritif

CLOUDY BAY PELORUS
Sparkling wine with aromas of fresh apple

Starters

PAUA FRITTERS
Mussel fritters with egg, onions, parsley and green salad

BLUFF OYSTERS
Fresh oysters from the Foveaux Strait off Stewart Island

Main courses

FISH PIE
A pie made from smoked fish, eggs and mashed potato with a crispy cheese crust

WHITEBAIT PATTIES
Transparent fish larvae and egg prepared as mini-omelettes with a crab-like flavour

FISH & CHIPS
Made with fresh blue cod and served with tartar sauce and cole slaw

BEEF, MUSHROOM & RED WINE PIE
Beef, mushrooms and red wine casserole, served with a fresh green salad

Desserts

HOKEY POKEY ICE CREAM
Vanilla ice cream with caramelized honey chunks

PIKELETS
Light mini-pancakes made from icing sugar and egg, served with whipped cream and jam

FRIANDS
A light almond cake with berries, served with natural yoghurt

Drinks

L&P (LEMON & PAEROA)
Classic New Zealand lemonade from Paeroa

PINOT ROSÉ
From the world's southernmost winery: Black Ridge in Otago

SHOPPING

100 % KIWI FASHION

Have you forgotten to pack your sunglasses? Not to worry, you can buy them from New Zealand designer Karen Walker, who creates fashionable frames in every imaginable colour and style. Lady Gaga, Debbie Harry and New Zealand singer Lorde are all fans of the brand.

Adrienne Whitewood is a talented designer who is inspired by Maori art and culture. She sells her clothes and baskets with traditional patterns in her Rotorua boutique.

The young fashion and jewellery label Company of Strangers from Dunedin is inspired by punk and rock music, and its collection is produced 100 per cent in New Zealand.

GREENSTONE

You can recognise New Zealanders worldwide from their jade necklaces.

You are not allowed to buy the *pounamu* (greenstone in Maori) yourself, but you should be given one as a gift. At least, that's the tradition. This is why jade is the perfect souvenir for friends and family. Typical Maori symbols are the fish hook *(Hei Matau)* or the spiral *(Koru)* which is reminiscent of an unfurling fern. You find *pounamu* especially in rivers around Hokitika on the west coast of South Island. The best greenstone artists also live here.

COOL ON THE BEACH

The sun's intensity is extreme in New Zealand. Nobody here spends the entire day on the beach in a bikini or swimming shorts; instead, they might wear a dress or T-shirt from surfer labels like Huffer from Auckland or RPM and Lower from Mount Maunganui. Piha Swimwear, named

Jade necklaces can only be bought as gifts, but you can buy yourself Karen Walker specs

after the famous surfer beach near Auckland, even sells bathing suits with long sleeves for added protection against sunburn.

NATURAL BEAUTY

Clear air, unspoilt nature and plants with unique healing powers: New Zealand is the perfect place for finding natural cosmetics. Honey from the manuka plant is full of proteins, vitamins and minerals, and is used in face creams. Considered a superfood for the skin, the black fern (mamaku) retains lots of mois-

INSIDER TIP
Anti-aging miracle bee venom

ture. Lotions with bee venom are said to stimulate the skin's collagen production and help to prevent wrinkles. Rotorua mud, from deep below New Zealand's earth, supplies minerals and makes the skin appear smoother. Certified

natural cosmetic brands from New Zealand are Wild Ferns, Living Nature, Moana, Trilogy and Oxygen Skincare.

DRESS FOR SOLITUDE

Fans of the great outdoors have a wide choice of good and reasonably priced outdoor shops in New Zealand. In Kathmandu outlets there are light down jackets and fleece pullovers in a variety of designs. Prices are generally reduced shortly after Christmas. You will feel perfectly equipped for trips into the wilderness in the softshell jackets and hiking boots from Mac Pac. Slightly more expensive, but of superior quality, are the locally produced, fair trade, merino wool jumpers from Glowing Sky on Stewart Island.

SPORT & ACTIVITIES

Kiwis are basically sporting mad, and that can be infectious. Climb mountains, take the plunge with the water sport of your choice or conquer New Zealand by bicycle.

ADVENTURE SPORTS

The steepest, fastest or craziest! Superlatives apply for everything in the native home of the bungy jump. Popular centres for this adrenalin rush are in the north in Rotorua and Taupo, in the south around Queenstown and Wanaka. *Jet Boats (tel. 0800 327 853 | dartriver.co.nz)* glide over the turquoise-coloured Dart River near Glenorchy. Beginners and pros can climb rock faces with *Wanaka Rock Climbing (tel. 022 015 4458 | wanaka rock.co.nz)*. Keep your eyes open during *Tandem Paragliding (tel. 0800 586 766 | skydivetaupo.co.nz)* over Taupo, as the panoramic views are incredible. If you prefer to float above the Earth, try *Freefall Extreme (tel. 0800 949 888 | velocityvalley.co.nz)* in Rotorua above a 220km/h wind tunnel. As preparation you can attend *Survival Training (tel. 0800 787 848 | sossurvivaltraining.com)* in the wilderness around Auckland.

CYCLING

An excellent cycle route network extends from New Zealand's mountainous north as far as the south; full information is available on *nzcycletrail. com*. You can enjoy one- and multiday tours with *Natural High (tel. 09 257 4673 | naturalhigh.co.nz)*; the support bus means you only ride on the most picturesque parts of the trail. Or you can ride 150km along an old train track on the *Otago Central Rail Trail (otagorailtrail.co.nz)*; it goes past a historic gold rush town and the never-ending panoramic views of South Island.

If bungy jumping isn't for you, explore the Queenstown countryside on horseback

Mountain bikers can test all their skills too: *nzcycletrail.com* and *trail forks.com* list countless trails. The legendary *42 Traverse*, for example, is an undulating 46-km trail through the forest and bush with views of North Island's volcanoes. The challenging *Old Ghost Trail (oldghostroad.org.nz)* along the wild west coast in the south is the country's longest trail and is only suitable for the fearless. Fans of the MTB course can test their skills on the *FourForty (fourfortymtbpark.co.nz)* in Auckland and in the *Cardrona Bike Park (cardrona.com)*, as well as on trails in the mountains around Queenstown. More information is available at *ridenz.co*. In New Zealand, you are required to wear a helmet, and remember, you always ride on the left!

DIVING

New Zealand is home to a whole host of marine life beneath the water's surface. The *Poor Knights Islands* off the coast of North Island, for example, attract tropical fish and stingrays and draw in visitors to their rock caves and steep rock faces *(diving courses: Dive! Tutukaka | tel. 09 434 3867 | diving.co.nz)*. Black coral grows in the deep waters of *Milford Sound (diving courses: Descend | tel. 02 7337 2363| descend.co.nz)* while the 2,000-m-deep ocean trench off the coast of *Kaikoura* is teeming with whales and other deep-sea creatures *(diving courses: Daves' Diving | tel. 021 0260 2316 | davesdivingkaikoura. com)*.

HIKING

You must register with the Department of Conservation *(doc.govt.nz/great-walks)* for any of the nine *Great*

Walks and book the huts in advance. In particular, the *Milford Track is* usually fully booked months ahead. If you prefer marathon hiking, you can trek the length of the entire country from north to south on the 3,000-km-long and well-integrated *Te Araroa – New Zealand's Trail (teararoa.org.nz).* There are shorter hiking trails around the country; these are listed on *freewalks.nz.*

HORSERIDING
Horseriding through breathtaking countryside is available countrywide for beginners and experienced riders. You can gallop with *Ahipara Horse Treks (tel. 09 408 2532 | taitokerau honey.co.nz)* across Ninety Mile Beach in Northland or across the bright white sand of *Pakiri Beach (tel. 09 422 6275 | horseride-nz.co.nz)* north of Auckland. In the impressive setting of mountains and lakes around *Queenstown (tel. 0800 236 566 | nzhorsetreks. co.nz)* you can enjoy fabulous views from horseback. Horse safaris off the beaten track that last for several days are available with *Alpine Horse Safaris (alpinehorse. co.nz)* in Canterbury. More information: *truenz.co.nz/horsetrekking.*

KAYAKING & CANOEING
Tranquil lakes, fast-flowing rivers and a varied coast offer fans of paddle sports ideal conditions almost anywhere in the country. On a canoe tour through *Pelorus Sound (canoe hire for 2 in Elaine Bay from NZ$100 | tel. 03 576 5251 | seakayakingmarlborough. co.nz)* on the northern tip of South Island you will escape civilisation after just a few strokes of the paddle and travel past unspoilt, secluded bays.

You will use every muscle in your body during a *kayak excursion (tel. 0800 999 089 | aucklandseakayaks. co.nz)* in Hauraki Gulf to Rangitoto followed by an ascent of the volcano.

KITESURFING & WINDSURFING
Two oceans close together, high mountains and rapidly changing weather: New Zealand is a paradise for wind-sports fanatics. You can learn kite- and windsurfing on the northern tip of South Island in Nelson *(tel. 0800 548 326 | kitescool.co.nz)* and in Auckland *(tel. 09 815 0683 | nzboard store.co.nz)* – with a west wind in Point Chevalier, or an east wind in Orewa. *windsurfingnz.org, FB: newzealand kitesurfing.*

SAILING
A good breeze is always blowing in the *Bay of Islands* and, naturally, in the City of Sails (Auckland). If you want to feel the air at the America's Cup, you can tame the winds on one of the speedy, high-tech boats in Auckland *(tel. 0800 397 567 | exploregroup. co.nz).* For a much gentler pace, you can try an *Akaroa Sailing Cruise (tel. 0800 724 528 | aclasssailing.co.nz)* near Christchurch.

SKIING
New Zealand's winter-sports centres generally have snow from June to

September. In the north, around the volcano *Ruapehu*, are the ski areas *Whakapapa* and *Turoa*. Ski hype is on the agenda – also snowboarding and heliskiing – in Queenstown *(queens townnz.co.nz)*, with the arenas at *Coronet Peak, Treble Cone, Cardrona* and *The Remarkables*. *Soho Basin (tel. 03 450 9098 | sohobasin.com)* near Cardrona is exclusive: a snow crawler or helicopter transports you to the slopes for untouched powdery snow. Over the mountain in neighbouring Wanaka, you will find New Zealand's only cross-country ski run *(snowfarm nz.com)*, and near Christchurch New Zealand's first eight-seater chairlift opened on *Mount Hutt* in 2021.

SUP & SURFING

Surfing is a lifestyle in New Zealand.

Riding the waves on stand-up paddle boards (SUP) is also increasingly popular. Most of the surfing hotspots are on North Island, and generally the east is tamer than the west. Popular surfing spots with boards for hire are *Piha* and *Muriwai* on Auckland's west coast, a little further south *Raglan* and along the *Surf Highway (SH 45)* in Taranaki. The top surfing spots on the east coast are in Northland around *Mangawhai* and in *Gisborne*. In the chilly south, among the favourites are *Sumner* in Christchurch and *St Clair* in Dunedin. Updated surfing weather forecasts are at *marineweather.co.nz* or *magicseaweed.com*. A tranquil SUP tour is possible in the protected bays and on many lakes, for example, *Lake Rotoiti* near Rotorua, the *Tutukaka Coast* or *Raglan Harbour*.

Long-distance cycling is a great way for fit visitors to explore the country

TASMAN
SEA

SOUTH ISLAND P. 86

Nelson

Greymouth

Hokitika

Franz Josef

Christchurch

Aoraki / Mount Cook

Lake Pukaki

Canterbury Bight

Lake Wakatipu

Few people, lots of sheep and nine national parks celebrating nature's wilderness

Queenstown

Te Anau

Dunedin

Invercargill

Foveaux Strait

100 km
62 mi

NORTH ISLAND p. 42

Maori culture, buzzing cities, dream beaches and subtropical vegetation

Auckland

Hamilton

Rotorua

Taupo

Gisborne

Napier

Whanganui

Hastings

Picton

WELLINGTON

Hauraki Gulf

Bay of Plenty

Lake Taupo

Hawke Bay

Cook Strait

PACIFIC OCEAN

NORTH ISLAND

SUBTROPICAL BEAUTY

You can decide for yourself how much of your holiday time you spend on each of New Zealand's main islands, but the whole country really deserves at least three weeks of your time. New Zealand's North Island is a beautiful region full of contrasts and with enough variety for your entire trip.

Explore the soft, white sandy beaches in the east and the black, wild coasts in the west of North Island. Discover Maori culture and the hustle and bustle of city life in the metropolises of Auckland

Laid-back New Zealand turns on the razzle-dazzle in Auckland

and Wellington. More adventurous visitors will love the steamy, volcanic heart of the north that is surrounded by beautiful lakes, rivers and forests.

Of course, the south has very impressive scenery too. However, it can get quite lonely there because more than two-thirds of New Zealand's population of 5.1 million live on North Island and most of them in the biggest city of Auckland. So, make sure you leave plenty of time for the people and enchanting beauty of North Island.

NORTH ISLAND

Cape Reinga  8

Ninety Mile Beach ★ 8

7
Ahipara

387km, 5 hrs 45 mins

Takaka

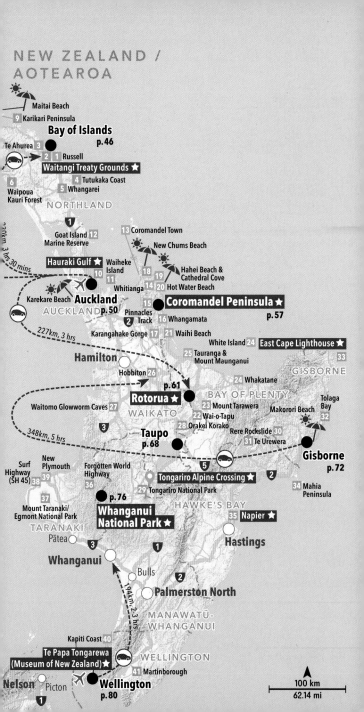

NEW ZEALAND / AOTEAROA

Maitai Beach
9 Karikari Peninsula
Bay of Islands p. 46
Te Ahurea **3**
2 **1** Russell
Waitangi Treaty Grounds ★
6 **4** Tutukaka Coast
Waipoua **5** Whangarei
Kauri Forest
NORTHLAND

13 Coromandel Town
Goat Island **12**
Marine Reserve
New Chums Beach
Hauraki Gulf ★ Waiheke
10 Island
11 **18** Hahei Beach &
19 Cathedral Cove
Whitianga **14** **20** Hot Water Beach
Karekare Beach **Auckland** p. 50
AUCKLAND **15** **Coromandel Peninsula** ★
Pinnacles **2** p. 57
Track **16** Whangamata
Karangahake Gorge **17** **21** Waihi Beach
White Island **24** **East Cape Lighthouse** ★
Hamilton **25** Tauranga & **33**
Mount Maunganui GISBORNE
Hobbiton **26** **24** Whakatane
p. 61 BAY OF PLENTY
Tolaga
Rotorua ★ **23** Mount Tarawera Bay
Makorori Beach
Waitomo Glowworm Caves **27** **22** Wai-o-Tapu **32**
WAIKATO **28** Orakei Korako
3 Rere Rockslide **30**
Taupo **31** Te Urewera
348km, 5 hrs p. 68 **5** **Gisborne**
p. 72
Surf New **34** Mahia
Highway Plymouth Forgotten World Peninsula
(SH 45) **38** **39** Highway **Tongariro Alpine Crossing** ★ **2**
36 **29** Tongariro National Park
37 **35** **Napier** ★
Mount Taranaki/ **p. 76**
Egmont National Park **Whanganui** HAWKE'S BAY
TARANAKI **National Park** ★
Pātea **Hastings**
3 **1**
Whanganui
Bulls
2
Palmerston North
MANAWATŪ-
WHANGANUI
Kapiti Coast **40**
Te Papa Tongarewa WELLINGTON
(Museum of New Zealand) ★
41 Martinborough
Nelson Picton **Wellington**
p. 80

100 km
62.14 mi

THE BAY OF ISLANDS

(🗺 H2–3) **This is a beautiful, picture-postcard idyll: green islands with white beaches and blue ocean. The 144 islands of the Bay of Islands are a paradise for sailors, sea fishermen and lovers of wildlife. Here, you can swim with dolphins, drop anchor in secluded bays or hike on solitary coastal paths.**

Most tours depart from Paihia (pop. 2,000), the bay's tourist centre. In Waitangi, you can learn all about the country's recent history, as this region is considered the cradle of modern New Zealand. Day-trip destinations are Ninety Mile Beach, ancient kauri forests, the remote Karikari Peninsula and Cape Reinga, the northern tip of New Zealand – the Northland is surrounded by deserted beaches.

SIGHTSEEING

◻ RUSSELL

The sleepy town (pop. 1,100) of today has a turbulent history. For a while, it was New Zealand's capital city and the rough customs of the whalers earnt it the name "Hell-hole of the Pacific". At *Christ Church (Robertson Road/ Church Street)*, which dates from 1835, you can still see the bullet holes of past battles. From *Flagstaff Hill* there is a fabulous view over the bay and at *Waterfront* you can enjoy a beer in a historic setting: the ⚑ *Duke of Marlborough (daily 11.30am–9pm | 35 The Strand | tel. 09 403 7829 | the duke.co.nz | $$–$$$ | also 25 rooms | $$$)* was the country's first pub licensed to serve alcohol. Today, you can also enjoy delicious food with a panoramic view towards Paihia, which is only a stone's throw away by ferry. 🗺 H3

◻ WAITANGI TREATY GROUNDS ★ ⚑

Here, the nation's adventurous beginnings are revived in a open-air-style museum. Five minutes outside Paihia, at the picturesque location where the state of New Zealand was originally founded, you will discover everything about the Waitangi Treaty.

The route to *Treaty House* leads through mangrove forests past a 35-m-long 150-man Maori war canoe made from two carved kauri tree-trunks. Every year in February the canoe is launched for the celebrations of *Waitangi Day*.

On the vast lawn area in front of Treaty House, on 6 February 1840, 50 Maori chiefs assembled with representatives of the English crown under the Governor of New Zealand, William Hobson, and signed the Waitangi Treaty that marked the country's rule by the British. The various controversial versions are displayed in *Waitangi Museum* at the entrance to the Treaty Grounds.

The impressive *Whare Runanga*, the Maoris' House of Assembly, with its carvings of ancestors from around the country, illustrates the regional unity of all the Maori tribes. There are Maori displays several times daily with Haka, as well as other dances and singing. *1 Feb–24 Dec daily 9am–5pm, 26 Dec–31 Jan daily 9am–6pm | NZ$60 including video, guided tour, show, museum | 1 Tau Henare Drive | waitangi.org.nz |* ⏱ *2 hrs | ▥ H3*

▣ TE AHUREA 🎭 🚩 🐃

The Maori village (formerly Rewa's Village) in Kerikeri – a living cultural centre – reopened in 2021 after extensive renovations costing over NZ$1 million. In the heart of the bush, visitors can take a trip back in time to experience how Maori people once lived, with courses in weaving and carving. There is even a *waka* (canoe) on the nearby Kerikeri River. *Tue–Sun 10am–5pm | NZ$10, children NZ$5 | 1 Landing Road | teahurea.co.nz |* ⏱ *2 hrs | ▥ H3*

EATING & DRINKING

Outside the main cities there is plenty of gastronomic variety. Paihia on the *Williams* and *Marsden Road* has the biggest choice. *Charlotte's Kitchen (daily from 11.30am | 69 Marsden Road | tel. 09 402 8296 | charlottes kitchen.co.nz | $$)* serves fresh fish, oysters and a whole host of Asian-inspired dishes. Just a few steps down the road is the small craft-beer bar *Thirty 30 (daily from 3pm | 16 Kings Road),* dishing up burgers, fish & chips and local beer while entertaining with live music.

SPORT & ACTIVITIES

BOAT TOURS

Getting out and about on the water is a must in the Bay of Islands. The

Art and nature combine at the open-air museum commemorating the Waitangi Treaty

Discover the Bay Cruise (daily 8.30am and 2pm | from NZ$135 | Marsden/corner of Williams Road | tel. 0800 365 744 | exploregroup.co.nz) leaves from Russell Wharf in Paihia. It is a half-day trip with plenty of highlights, including the *Hole in the Rock* gate that you can tour by boat in fine weather and with a lunch or swimming stop on the breathtakingly beautiful *Urupukapuka Island*.

If you prefer to swim with dolphins, 🐋 *Carina Sailing (daily 9am from Paihia | from NZ$140, children NZ$97 | tel. 09 402 8040 | sailingdolphins. co.nz)* offers a six-hour catamaran sailing tour with snorkelling and barbecue. If dolphins are spotted, you can jump into the water. Or you can relax on deck and admire the marine animals' amazing acrobatics.

BEACHES

For the most beautiful beaches, head to the north of the Bay of Islands to Ahipara and the Karikari Peninsula.

WELLNESS

NGAWHA SPRINGS

The warm thermal water that fills the 16 pools at Ngawha Springs in Kaikohe (80km from Russell) has its sources deep in the Earth. Rich in minerals, it is said to have healing properties. The pool reopened in 2022 following renovation. *283 Ngawha Springs Road | tel. 09 405 2245 | ngawha.nz*

AROUND THE BAY OF ISLANDS

4 TUTUKAKA COAST

90km/1 hr 15 mins from Pahia (car)

If you like the coast, you will love this coastline north of Auckland. For divers and snorkellers, the marine conservation area on *Poor Knights Islands* is simply breathtaking. The water around the volcanic islands is super clear and in summer it warms up to 23°C. In addition to 120 native fish species, dolphins and giant kelp (brown seaweed) gardens, you might, if you're lucky, see other tropical species such as manta rays or even whale sharks.

Along the islands' rocky coastline, you can discover unique underwater plants, reefs and the Rikoriko Cave: you can explore the world's biggest sea cave with kayaks or paddle boards. *Excursion boats (daily 11am–4.15pm | NZ$229 | tel. 0800 288 882 | aperfect day.co.nz)* depart daily from Tutukaka Marina to the islands about 20km off the picturesque east coast. Take plenty of time to explore the Tutukaka Coast where you'll find secluded green coves like *Matapouri Bay* and the excellent surf beach *Sandy Bay*. 🔲 *H3*

5 WHANGAREI

70km/1 hr from Pahia (car)

A detour to this harbour town will certainly be worth your while, not just because of the beautiful waterfront

The Bay of Islands encompasses 144 individual pockets of blue and green paradise

but also thanks to the new *Hundertwasser Art Centre*. The museum, which opened in early 2022, boasts the largest Hundertwasser collection outside Vienna. It pays tribute to the Austrian artist, who spent the last 25 years of his life in New Zealand. The Kawakawa Toilets were his largest work of art to make its mark on the country. *Mon–Sat 10am–5pm, Sun until 4pm | NZ$21 | 81 Dent Street | h u n d e r t w a s s e r a r t centre.co.nz | ⊙ 1.5 hrs | ⊞ H3*

6 WAIPOUA KAURI FOREST 🚩

120km/1 hr 45 mins from Pahia (car)
Standing beneath the oldest and biggest kauri tree *Tane Mahuta*, the "God of the Forest", (51m tall, 14-m circumference, and an estimated 2,000 years old), you will feel very insignificant. The west coast of

Northland is still regarded as Kauri Coast, even if most of these ancient giants were cut down by European settlers in about 1860. Explore the forest under your own steam or book a tour with a Maori guide at *Footprints Waipoua (daily | price on request | tel. 09 405 8207 | footprintswaipoua.co.nz)*. Especially impressive is the four-hour night tour (NZ$105), where you adventure almost

all alone into the forest on a journey back in time to the New Zealand of a thousand years ago. Your guide will retell ancient legends and sing Maori songs to bring the past to life. The *Kauri Museum (daily 9am–6pm | NZ$25 | 5 Church Road | kaurimuseum. com | ⊙ 30 mins)* in Matakohe explains the history of the trees that are protected under nature conservation. ⊞ G3

7 AHIPARA

120km/1 hr 45 mins from Pahia (car)
This is a surfers' paradise northwest of Paihia. *Ninety Mile Beach* begins below the town in *Shipwreck Bay*. The bay is like a surfers' car park on days when the surf is high. Hardcore surfers drive even further along the rocky coast where one big surfing spot follows another. It's best not to try this in a rental car as they are not insured here or on the beach. However, at low tide you can drive along the endless sandy beach in sand buggies. But you should always keep an eye on the tides! *G3*

8 CAPE REINGA & NINETY MILE BEACH

200km/2 hrs 30 mins from Pahia to Cape Reinga (car)
According to Maori legend, on New Zealand's northernmost tip, at *Cape Reinga*, the souls of the departed live on and continue their journey to the afterlife. The cape is a mythical place, and the desert landscape makes for incredible 😎 *dune surfing with the kids*. Boogie boards can be rented once you get there.

The Pacific and Tasman Sea meet at Cape Reinga and the view from the local *lighthouse* is awe-inspiring. It's best to book an 11-hour tour from Paihia to so-called Northland, e.g. with *Great Sights (daily 7am | NZ$160 | tel. 0800 744 487 | greatsights.co.nz)*. The trip is long and, for the last 90km the endless, usually empty ★ *Ninety Mile Beach* lines the route. The tour buses also travel along the beach – including a sandboarding stop. The fantastic

Ninety Mile Beach is, in fact, only 88km (55 miles) long – not quite as long as its name suggests. *F-G2*

9 KARIKARI PENINSULA

110km/1 hr 30 mins from Pahia (car)
The *Karikari Peninsula* is no man's land: long, white, sandy beaches and behind them sand dunes and lagoons. There are also a few small towns, a wine estate and olive groves. Kite surfers love this flat peninsula north of Paihia as it's always windy on one of the coasts. *Rangiputa* is situated on a flat lagoon which is perfect for beginners and keen fishermen. The wonderful, crescent-shaped ⭐ *Maitai Beach* on the northern tip of the peninsula embraces the protected bay with the same name. Meanwhile, the sea at *Matauri Bay* is particularly turquoise.

AUCKLAND

(H–J5) **The location on the wonderful Hauraki Gulf characterises Auckland and its people, who are relaxed, positive and open-minded. In general, locals rarely allow things to bother them.**

Auckland is situated on the narrowest land strip between the Pacific Ocean to the east and the Tasman Sea to the west, which can influence the constantly changing weather conditions. A fresh breeze always blows in the "City of Sails", so the harbour is always busy with sailing boats. With a population of 1.7 million, New

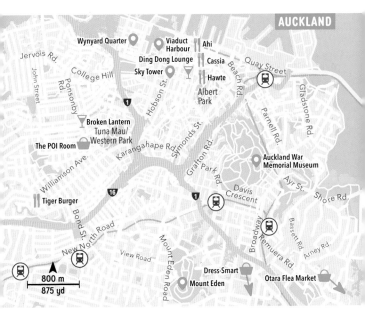

AUCKLAND

Wynyard Quarter
Viaduct Harbour
Ahi
Jervois Rd.
College Hill
Ding Dong Lounge
Cassia
Beach Rd.
Quay Street
Sky Tower
Hawte
John Street
Ponsonby Rd.
Hobson St.
Albert Park
Gladstone Rd.
Broken Lantern
Tuna Mau/
Western Park
Symonds St.
Parnell Rd.
The POI Room
Karangahape Rd.
Grafton Rd.
Auckland War Memorial Museum
Williamson Ave.
Park Rd.
Ayr St.
Davis Crescent
Shore Rd.
Tiger Burger
Bond St.
New North Road
Mount Eden Road
View Road
Bowden Rd.
Bassett Rd.
Remuera Rd.
Arney Rd.
800 m
875 yd
Dress-Smart
Mount Eden
Otara Flea Market

Zealand's biggest city was founded in 1840 and became the capital for a few years before Wellington became the seat of government in 1865. To this day, there is rivalry between the two cities, although the focus is mainly on sporting results and the number of cafés.

Auckland has many culinary highlights, mainly in the sophisticated wharf district and in Ponsonby. Every city quarter has its own multicultural charm: the southern districts reflect a Pacific flair while commercial Queen Street reveals Asian influences. Thanks to over 50 (extinct) volcanoes, the city is hilly and has plenty of green spaces. Forty minutes from the centre you can go surfing in the west on a wild, black sandy beach in the morning and enjoy a lazy afternoon on the white sandy beaches of the east side in the afternoon.

SIGHTSEEING

SKY TOWER

"The Needle", as the the Sky Tower is also known, is Auckland's icon on the

---

WHERE TO START?

Sky Tower: Enjoy the best city views from a height of 382m! Starting at the tower, you can explore the city centre on foot; the Wynyard Quarter waterfront is just a few steps away. The first hour is free at the Jellicoe Street Car Park (Beaumont Street) and afterwards costs NZ$6/hr.

The undulating summit of Mount Eden indicates its volcanic origins

city's skyline. The lift (NZ$25) transports you in 40 seconds to the viewing platform 220m above street level. There is a casino, bars and the revolving *Orbit* restaurant *(daily from 11.30am | minimum charge! | tel. 09 363 6000 | $$–$$$)* with 360-degree panoramic views. The *SkyJump (from NZ$135)* from the tower is best undertaken before dinner (certainly from the point of view of passers-by!). Slightly less adventurous, but with the same dizzy views, is the *SkyWalk (from NZ$90)* around the top of the tower – please note, it's outside! *Daily from 8.30 am | Victoria Street | skycity auckland.co.nz*

WYNYARD QUARTER & VIADUCT HARBOUR

The modern harbour districts of *Wynyard Quarter (wynyard-quarter. co.nz)* and *Viaduct Harbour (viaduct.*

co.nz), with their stylish architecture, are places to see and be seen. Enjoy a stroll through the residential and leisure quarter by the waterfront, treat yourself to an excellent meal in the modern *Soul Bar (daily from 11am | tel. 09 356 7249 | soulbar.co.nz | $$–$$$)* with views of the enviable luxury yachts in Viaduct Harbour. A bascule bridge leads further into Wynyard Quarter, where you can enjoy more reasonably priced and artisan food. In summer, in the adjacent ✿ *Silo Park (silopark.co.nz)* open-air films are screened free of charge.

AUCKLAND WAR MEMORIAL MUSEUM 🕊

This museum provides an introduction to New Zealand's culture, from the Pacific settlers to the modern period. The impressive neoclassical building with panoramic views of the city is also the war memorial to fallen soldiers. It is on the site of an old crater – today, one of the largest city parks with beautiful old trees and plenty of green spaces. The Maori exhibitions in Rotorua or the Bay of Islands are more authentic, so you might want to opt out of this one. But you should definitely visit the *Wintergarden (daily from 9am | free admission | Wintergarden Road)* in the grounds of the museum with its collection of native ferns. *Mon–Fri 10am–5pm, Sat/Sun 9am–5pm | NZ$28 | Auckland Domain | aucklandmuseum.com | ⏱ 1.5 hrs*

MOUNT EDEN

When you see the sheep grazing on the green slopes of this former volcano you can't imagine how hot things get below: the *Auckland Volcanic Field* just below the surface is still active. The question is not whether but when the next volcano will erupt. But don't worry, there should be a few years to go yet. From the edge of the crater of the city's highest volcano (196m) there is a fantastic view. Maungawhau – the Maori name for Mount Eden – is a sacred place for the local Maori people, so visitors should behave respectfully and not venture into the crater. *Summer daily 7am–8.30pm; winter daily 7am–7pm | 250 Mount Eden Road*

EATING & DRINKING

AHI 🚩

Head chef Ben Bay is a true pioneer when it comes to the skillet. He experiments in his award-winning restaurant with traditional Maori cooking techniques, serving up octopus with pikopiko fern tips or blackberries with honey from the pohutukawa tree. Diners, meanwhile, can work up an appetite on sea-blue velvet chairs with a view of Queen Street as they wait for their edible works of art. *Daily, noon–midnight | 7/21 Queen Street | tel. 02 2524 4255 | ahirestaurant.co.nz | $$–$$$*

CASSIA

The finest cuisine! Modern fusion with various Asian influences – one of the city's best restaurants, also a groovy cellar location near the Britomart (station). *Lunch Wed and Thu 12.30–2.30pm, dinner Tue–Sat from 5.30pm | 5 Fort Lane | tel. 09 379 9702 | cassiarestaurant.co.nz | $$–$$$*

TIGER BURGER

Asian-inspired burgers are the latest food trend to hit Auckland. What can we say? Kimchi or Korean spices with beef are a match made in heaven. We promise it's worth the queue at Tiger Burger in trendy Grey Lynn to order a "kimcheese" with kimchi, locally sourced organic beef and cheddar cheese. There are plenty of options for vegetarians, too. *Tue–Fri 5–9pm, Sat/Sun noon–9pm | 549 Great North Road | tel. 09 216 5585 | tigerburger.co.nz | $*

SHOPPING

Around *Queen Street* you can shop to your heart's content: fashion, outdoor wear, electronics, souvenir shops and supermarkets. You will find designer fashion and handicrafts on *Lorne Street*, in the *Britomart District* near the station and on *Ponsonby Road*. New Zealand's biggest shopping centre at *Sylvia Park* in Mount Wellington offers a compact shopping experience with more than 200 shops.

DRESS-SMART

For bargain hunters – New Zealand's biggest outlet mall has a good selection of fashion and sports shops, maybe not with the absolute latest fashions but heavily discounted. Tourists benefit from a free shuttle to Onehunga located 30 minutes way – see the timetable at *dress-smart.co.nz*. *Mon–Wed, Fri 10am–5pm, Sat/Sun 9am–6pm | 151 Arthur Street*

OTARA FLEA MARKET

A busy flea market Polynesian style with live music and South Sea atmosphere. Tongans, Samoans, Fijians and Maoris are represented with their food, jewellery, clothing and vegetable stalls. A truly multicultural experience. *Sat 6am–noon | Newbury Street | Manukau*

THE POI ROOM

The Poi Room offers authentic New Zealand arts and crafts, jewellery and souvenirs – produced by local artists. Authenticity comes at a price, but the tasteful products are exclusive and original. *Mon–Fri 10am–5.30pm, Sat 10am–5pm, Sun 10am–4pm | 130 Ponsonby Road*

SPORT & ACTIVITIES

KELLY TARLTON'S SEALIFE AQUARIUM

Plexiglass tunnels lead through aquariums to showcase New Zealand's underwater world. *Daily 9.30am–5pm | adults NZ$39, children over 3 years NZ$27, under 3s free | 23 Tamaki Drive | Auckland | kellytarltons.co.nz | ⏲ 2 hrs*

SURFING

The wild west coast beaches with their black sand are not for cautious swimmers. *Piha* and *Muriwai* are considered the best surfing spots in the country. Beginners should learn the art of surfing the waves from the pros at the *surf schools (pihasurfschool.com, muriwaisurfschool.co.nz)*; the boards and wetsuits are also for hire here. Top tip: here in the west, surfing at sunset is just great!

WILDLIFE WATCH

Orcas in front of the ferry terminal and dolphins racing alongside yachts – all kinds of marine animals, even humpback whales and Bryde's whales appear here in the nutrient-rich Hauraki Gulf. The informative, roughly five-hour *whale-watching tour* with *Auckland Whale & Dolphin Safari (daily 10.15am | NZ$129, children NZ$89 | 175 Quay Street | Viaduct Harbour | tel. 09 357 6032 | whalewatchingauckland.com)* comes with a guarantee: if you don't glimpse any marine mammals, you can join a second tour.

Regal shopping on Queen Street

BEACHES

Perfect for families, *Orewea Beach* is 3km long with gentle swells and is roughly 30 minutes from downtown Auckland by car. Children are free to potter in the sand and swim in the shallow water without being disturbed. Forty-five minutes from the city centre, *Karekare Beach* (made famous by Jane Campion's film *The Piano*) promises wild beauty. Over in *Takapuna*, a district of Auckland, films are shown for free on the beach during the summer.

IKOI SPA

Relax and rejuvenate all in one go. Try a massage, facial or enzyme treatment at the Japanese Ikoi Spa in Auckland's pretty Takapuna district, complete with sandy white beaches. *Tue–Sun 10am–8pm | 1 Huron Street | tel. 09 489 1818 | ikoispa.co.nz*

NIGHTLIFE

Pubs and bars are located within walking distance of the harbour: around the *Britomart (station)*, *Viaduct Harbour*, *Wynyard Quarter* and in trendy *Ponsonby*.

DING DONG LOUNGE

The home of rock 'n' roll. DJs play grunge, punk and rock in the basement, while New Zealand's top bands take to the first-floor stage every week from Wed–Sat at the *Dead Witch Bar*. *Tue–Sat 6pm–4am | 26 Wyndham Street | dingdongloungenz.com*

INSIDER TIP
Kiwi rock at full volume

BROKEN LANTERN

Drink in style as award-winning bartenders mix negronis and mojitos in a cool speakeasy-inspired ambience. Craft beer on tap and pizza and burgers available for indulgence. *Wed–Thu 4pm–1am, Fri–Sun from noon | 198 Ponsonby Road | broken-lantern.co.nz*

AROUND AUCKLAND

🔟 HAURAKI GULF ★

12km/15 mins from Auckland (car)
This giant water playground right by the "City of Sails" extends as far as Coromandel Peninsula. Several marine conservation areas and about 50 islands are dotted around the gulf. Close by is *Rangitoto*, the city's undisputed natural monument and the newest of Auckland's volcanoes. The last eruption was about 600 years ago. The *half-day trip (NZ$39 | fullers.co.nz)* to the island is a combination of pleasant boat trip followed by the ascent of the crater (260m, approx. one hour) through New Zealand's biggest Pohutukawa forest and past a lava cave. From the summit the view over Auckland and the gulf makes a 360-degree panoramic picture well worthwhile. *J4–5*

🔟 WAIHEKE ISLAND

40km/40 mins from Auckland (ferry)
Waiheke Island is the perfect place for gourmets and slow travellers. The second biggest island in the gulf with an area of approx. 90km² has green hills, small bays, vineyards and some amazing houses. A mixture of rich and alternative Aucklanders live on Waiheke. *Ecozipadventures.co.nz* offers the three-hour *Island tour (NZ$129)* including a superfast zipline and nature trail. Afterwards, simply stop off at one of the wonderful vineyards – e.g. at *Cable Bay Vineyards (cablebay.nz)* – where the delicious *lunch platters* will complement the magnificent view. More information is available at *waiheke.co.nz*.

The ferries to the islands in the gulf depart several times daily *(details at fullers.co.nz)*. If you prefer time travel, you should join the three-hour ferry excursion *(sealink.co.nz)* to *Great Barrier Island* (see p. 143). You will discover New Zealand as it was 40 years ago, with lush vegetation, beaches and not many people. Paradise! *J5*

🔟 GOAT ISLAND MARINE RESERVE

85km/1 hr 10 mins from Auckland (car)
Put on the fins and diving mask, open your eyes and set off around Goat Island near Leigh to snorkel with ancient snappers (the bigger they are the older they are – and the ones here are really big!). North of Auckland is New Zealand's oldest marine conservation area directly on a narrow beach. The island itself is a nature reserve and entry is not permitted. Kayak and snorkel hire *(goatislanddive.co.nz)* is available on the beach. The *Goat Island Discovery Centre (Daily*

Goat Island is a great place to go diving off the coast of Auckland

10am–4pm | NZ$9 | 160 Goat Island Road | goatislandmarine.co.nz | ⏱ 30 mins) up the hill has an interesting interactive exhibition about the marine conservation area. 🔲 J4

COROMANDEL PENINSULA

(🔲 J–K5) **Sand between your toes and in every crevice (of your car) – a trip to the beach is a must when visiting this beautiful peninsula.** ★

Whitianga is an ideal starting point to explore the bays along the northeast coast. A little further south around Whangamata, the wonderful surf beaches are inviting, and in the west

the protected sea estuary of the Thames creates excellent conditions for seabirds to spend the winter. In the middle of all this are relics of the gold-diggers in a ravine surrounded by a green mountain chain. The gravel roads in the northern part of Coromandel offer adventurers with their own car magical panoramic vistas of the coasts below.

SIGHTSEEING

🔟 COROMANDEL TOWN

A magnet for hippies and arty types – the sleepy place on the peninsula's west coast has a few cafés and galleries and pretty little houses in colonial style. The gallery of Barry Brickell, a potter who died in 2016, is legendary along with his 🚂 *Driving Creek Railway (daily 10.30am, 11.15am,*

Potter through the reforested landscape on the Driving Creek Railway

12.45pm, 2.15pm, 3.45pm, 4.30pm, 6pm | NZ$37, children NZ$15 | book in advance | 380 Driving Creek Road | tel. 07 866 8703 | drivingcreek.nz) – a rustic narrow-gauge railway through the regenerated New Zealand forest. It was a personal project created by the talented nature conservationist. The one-hour journey passes sculptures and crosses viaducts. Part of the ticket price is dedicated to reforestation. There is also a café. ▥ *J5*

⓮ WHITIANGA

With a little luck, in this paradise for sea fishermen, you will see a giant blue marlin (about 3m long!) with its long spear, when the fishing boats land with their catch at the marina.

If you prefer to see fish on your plate, you're in the right place in Whitianga. *Stoked Bar & Restaurant (Fri–Sun noon–9pm, Thu from 5pm | 19 The Esplanade | tel. 07 866 0029 | getstoked.co.nz | $–$$)* serves fresh tiger prawns and green-lipped mussels overlooking Mercury Bay. f *J5*

⓯ PINNACLES TRACK

A challenging day's hike in the trekking paradise of *Kauaeranga Valley*, east of the Thames has many rewards! The scenery is magnificent and the panoramic vista from the 759-m-tall pinnacles is breathtaking – although you may be out of breath anyway after the four-hour ascent through the dense Nikau palm forest crossing streams and rope bridges. After about three hours, you can enjoy a short break at the well-equipped Department of Conservation (DOC) hut. The last 40 minutes to the summit are adventurous – chains and ladders help you over the dramatic rock formations. The descent is less challenging, but your knees will appreciate the support of walking sticks. You can trek up and down the same route or you can stop overnight in the DOC hut (*Pinnacles Hut | 80 beds | NZ$25/night | book in advance online! | doc.govt.nz*) and travel back via the *Billygoat Tramline* on an old logger's path. ▢ *J5*

16 WHANGAMATA

Here, on the east coast of Coromandel, halfway between Waihi and Hot Water Beach, everyone runs around in surf shorts and flip-flops – authentic Kiwi beach life with sand, waves and a pleasant café scene in the town. *Blackies Café (daily 7.30am–3pm | 418 Ocean Road | tel. 07 865 9834 | $)* near the beach is popular with the locals, not least probably because of the super-friendly service.

On a stand-up paddle tour to Donut Island, which is actually called *Whenuakura Island*, you soon get that Robinson Crusoe feeling. On this round island, there are no sweet pastries, but right in the centre a turquoise-coloured lagoon that you enter through a rocky portal. *Surfsup New Zealand (2 hrs | NZ$68 | tel. 02 1217 1201 | surfsup.nz)* offers a guided tour on a paddle board. ▢ *K5*

17 KARANGAHAKE GORGE

Elves or hobbits would feel at home in the green mountain landscape around Karangahake Gorge, which connects Waihi and Paeroa in the south of Coromandel Peninsula. There are fairy-tale views to the fern-covered valley of the Ohinemuri River. From 1870 to 1950, there were four gold mines in this area. On the *Karangahake Tunnel Walk (start at Karangahake car park at SH2)* you can hike at your own pace along the old tracks used to transport gold through the lush vegetation and the 1-km old railway tunnel. You can feel like *Lord of the Gold Rings!* ▢ *J5*

EATING & DRINKING

COROMANDEL MUSSEL KITCHEN

Green-lipped mussels straight from the Thames estuary. A hearty beer garden atmosphere with home-brewed beer

INSIDER TIP
A toast for the gold rush

from the MK-Brewery, e.g. *Gun Smoke Ale* or *Gold Digger Pils*. 10 minutes from Coromandel Town. *Tue–Thu, Sun 10am–4pm, Fri/Sat until 8pm | 20 309 Road/corner of Manaia Road (SH25) | tel. 07 866 7727 | mussel kitchen.co.nz | $-$$* ▢ *J5*

MANAIA

The stone-baked pizza is exceptional. Fish, meat and vegetarian dishes complete the offers. Popular with locals and tourists. *Daily from 12pm | 228 Main Road | Tairua | tel. 07 864 9050 | manaia.co.nz | $$* ▢ *K5*

Create your own hot tub on Hot Water Beach

BEACHES

🔟 NEW CHUMS BEACH

Wow! Thirty minutes north from Whangapoua is this golden beach surrounded by forest and lapped by the incredibly clear water of Wainuiototo Bay. New Chums is among New Zealand's top ten beaches for a reason, even if it is a bit off the beaten track in the northern part of the Coromandel Peninsula. *J4*

🔟 HAHEI & CATHEDRAL COVE

From the long, white, sandy beach in *Hahei* on the peninsula's east side, there is a wonderful two-hour coastal hike to picturesque *Cathedral Cove* with its towering, cathedral-like limestone formations in the sea. If you kayak to the bay (*various tours from*

Hahei Beach | tel. 0800 529 258 | kayak tours.co.nz), you can avoid the crowded coastal path and have an impressive view of the rocky coast from below. Parking in Hahei in the peak season can be a nightmare. A shuttle departs from the car park at the entrance to the town to the start of the Cathedral Cove Walkways. *K5*

🔟 HOT WATER BEACH

On Hot Water Beach you can dig your very own hot pool with a sea view – the deeper, the hotter, so they say. You can rent spades for about NZ$5. If the sand bubbling from the thermal water gets too hot, simply cool off in the surf – a wellness spa New Zealand style. You should start your pool-digging at the earliest two hours before or at the latest two hours after low tide, otherwise you will be relaxing with a snorkel! It's also best to treat this as a social experience, since you are guaranteed plenty of pool neighbours. Next to the beach car park you'll find a cute *art and design gallery and workshop (FB: MokoArt space).* 🗺 *K5*

21 WAIHI BEACH

Fifteen minutes from Waihi, which is rather dreary, is this extremely long, sandy beach. From the 45-minute *hiking path* the views over dreamy Orokawa Bay are impressive. Simply park at the northern end of the beach and trek uphill. 🗺 *K5*

WELLNESS

THE LOST SPRING

This stunning spa oasis in Whitianga could easily be a kitsch waterfall poster from the 1980s. Hidden in dense rainforest, the water in the pools flows from a depth of 600m and is chock-full of minerals. As if a dip in this natural wonder weren't enough, the site also boasts a bar, spa area and restaurant. Booking required. *Fri/Sat 9.30am–9pm, Sun until 7pm | 121 A Cook Drive | tel. 07 866 0456 | thelostspring.co.nz |* 🗺 *J5*

NIGHTLIFE

The Pour House (Mon–Fri 5–9pm, Sat/ Sun from 12pm | 7 Grange Road | thepourhouse.co.nz) is a trendy pub in Haihei complete with a pleasant beer garden and its own brewery. *Good as gold* craft beer and local wines are complemented by pizza and seafood.

The summer concerts at the *Coroglen Tavern (Tue–Sun from 12pm | 1937 Tairua Whitianga Road | coroglen tavern.co.nz)* in the village of the same name, meanwhile, have become the stuff of legend. Famous Kiwi bands like Shapeshifter or SixSixty have graced the boards of the open-air stage here.

ROTORUA

(🗺 *K6*) **There is steam, hissing and bubbling and a smell of rotten eggs. Hold your nose and carry on because the geothermal phenomena in this region can leave behind a truly explosive impression.**

⭐ Rotorua is located in the highly active *Taupo Volcanic Zone* and is also the country's Maori heartland. The ancestors of the Te Arawa people are said to have belonged to the first people in New Zealand and today their descendents are very proud of their culture. In Rotorua, the Maoris take the lead when it comes to tourism. Most of the major tourism companies and the region's thermal parks are run by Te Arawa people. While the typical cultural performances are in some ways "for show", they still give an authentic portrayal of their vibrant culture. The city on Lake Rotorua is surrounded by pine forests, dormant volcanoes and lakes. Obviously, the location (pop. 71,700) is a tourist magnet: "Rotovegas" offers the full New Zealand programme of nature, culture and adventure sports.

SIGHTSEEING

GOVERNMENT GARDENS & ROTORUA MUSEUM

Manicured gardens and English lawns honour the horticultural motherland in the Government Gardens. 🐖 *Free guided tours* of the beautiful gardens take place daily at 11am and 2pm *(book by phone on 02 72 42 41 32).*

The former city spa is today a showcase for the culture of the Te Arawa people and the history of the old bathing house. The attractive Elizabethan-style building with its half-timbered façade and distinctive red roofs feels like something from a children's fairy tale on a grand scale. *As of the time of press, the building was closed due to earthquake repairs; it is scheduled to reopen in late 2025 | Government Gardens | rotorua museum.co.nz*

LAKE ROTORUA

Lake Rotorua is North Island's second largest lake and, like most of the lakes in this region, it was the caldera of a volcanic eruption about 140,000 years ago. *Mokoia Island* at the centre of the lake is a nature conservation area and a sacred place for the Maoris as well as being surrounded by a legendary love story. Because her father had forbidden Hinemoa to canoe to the island, where her beloved Tutanekai was waiting, she swam the 3km and followed the sound of the flute, which Tutanekai was playing. Today, the journey to the island is easy and fast with the *K-Jet Watertaxi (daily | NZ$119 incl. guided tour and visit to the hot pools | tel. 0800 538 7746 | nzjetboat.co.nz).*

SKYLINE ROTORUA 😝

From the gondola you can enjoy the view over the city and lake with a really generous New Zealand buffet. To add to the excitement, you might enjoy the return trip on the luge. *Daily 9am–10pm | from NZ$35 | 178 Fairy Springs Road | tel. 07 347 0027 | skyline.co.nz/rotorua | Dinner $$$*

WHAKAREWAREWA & TE PUIA 😝

The undisputed full programme in Rotorua: here, you can discover the extensive thermal region of *Whakarewarewa* (Whaka for short) as well as the spiritual and cultural centre of the Maori people, *Te Puia*. The *Marae* (assembly place), *Waka* (warriors' canoe) and *Pa* (permanent village) offer impressive examples of Maori architecture. The shows with traditional Maori customs are informative and entertaining: from *Powhiri*, the welcome ceremony, and *Poi*, the women's dance, to the famous 🚩 *Haka*, the warrior dance that includes sticking out tongues to intimidate the opponents. Things are a lot calmer in the *New Zealand Maori Arts and Crafts Institute*, where you can watch Maori artisans as they weave and carve.

Whaka's geothermal highlight is the 30m spraying geyser known as *Pohutu*, not surprisingly, meaning "explosion". In the 1970s the geyser's energy was siphoned off and the thermal energy was used for traditional heating and cooking, but this is

Discover the spiritual and cultural heart of the Maori people at Te Puia

now regulated. The Te Puia package includes boiling mud pools, hot stones and a Kiwi Nighthouse. Guided tours (on the hour) are included in the price; the guides are members of the local Maori tribe. There are good, combined packages that include guided tour, show and buffet with *hangi*, the hearty and traditional Maori dish prepared and cooked in ovens under the ground. *Hangi* contains kumara (sweet potato), root vegetables and fish, chicken or lamb braised for three to four hours in the natural heat of the earth. It's plentiful and satisfying food! *Daily 8am–6pm, in winter until 5pm | from NZ$54 for a day tour with various booking options, night tours also available | Hemo Road | tel. 0800 405 623 | tepuia.com*

Tamaki Maori Village (daily 5pm, 6.15pm and 7.30pm | NZ$130 | tel. 05 *0882 6254 | tamakimaorivillage. co.nz)* also offers a worthwhile three-hour cultural evening show with shuttle and *hangi* buffet. As a glimmering bonus you can see glow-worms on a short bush walk. Shuttle service from the hotel.

EATING & DRINKING

CAPERS
Centrally located café serving an excellent breakfast and mouthwatering specialities such as lamb in rosemary sauce and lemon tart for dessert. Not exactly cheap, but delicious. *Daily 7am–7pm | 1181 Eruera Street | tel. 07 348 8818 | capers.co.nz | $$–$$$*

TERRACE KITCHEN
Relaxed restaurant with unbeatable service and a central lakeside location.

Home-made light snacks in the day; in the evening, heartier dishes such as New Zealand lamb or the fresh catch of the day. *Daily from 7.30am | 1029 Tutanekai Street | tel. 07 460 1229 | terrace.kitchen | $–$$$*

SHOPPING

Souvenirs such as typical New Zealand pendants, lucky charms with Maori symbols made from whale bones or jade are everywhere here. But make sure you check the origin of the jade: is it from China or New Zealand? The Maori experts at *Puawai Jade (daily 10am–5pm | 1174 Whakaue Street | puawaijade.nz)* carve their own gems from the local greenstone. They also offer a tour behind the scenes at the workshop.

SPORT & ACTIVITIES

CANOPY TOURS

Swing like Tarzan through the treetops of ancient, native New Zealand forest. This is a rarity in a country where the first settlers made sure of almost total deforestation. Part of your money for the three-hour tour over bridges and walkways with ziplines up in the tree canopy goes to support the operator's nature conservation programme. *Daily 8am–8pm, winter to 6pm | NZ$159, children NZ$129 | 147 Fairy Springs Road | tel. 0800 226 679 | canopytours.co.nz*

MOUNTAIN BIKES IN THE REDWOODS

East of Rotorua in the magnificent Redwoods, 130km of mountainous

See, hear, feel and smell the geothermal activity in Rotorua

trail await you in the Whakarewarewa Forest around the beautiful blue and green lakes. There are different terrains, levels of difficulty and distances. Mountain bikes are available for hire in Rotorua from *Mountain Bike Rotorua (daily 9am–5pm | from NZ$39 for 2 hrs | tel. 0800 682 768 | mtbrotorua.co.nz)*. More information: *Redwoods I-Site & Visitor Information Centre (Long Mile Road | redwoods.co.nz)*. Next to the visitor centre you can also go on a *Treewalk (daily 9am–10pm | NZ$35)* through the Redwoods – also with floodlighting in the evenings.

WELLNESS

POLYNESIAN SPA 🌴

You deserve some relaxation! One of the oldest, but also most modern spa amenities in the town on Lake Rotorua benefits from various thermal springs. There are larger pools, private pools and family-sized pools. You can also enjoy some treatments – e.g. mud massages. A private pool under a star-lit sky in winter is especially romantic. *Daily 8am–11pm | private pool for 2 from NZ$50 | 1000 Hinemoa Street | tel. 07 348 1328 | polynesianspa.co.nz*

KUIRAU PARK 🐗

Treat your tired feet to a hot bath and chat with the locals in Rotorua's only public thermal park with mud pools, a small crater lake and hot springs. Always be sure to stay on the cold side of the fences! This is rustic thermal relaxation in the city centre. *Free access | Lake Road/corner of Ranolf Street*

AROUND ROTORUA

22 WAI-O-TAPU

30km/25 mins from Rotorua (car)
Poisonous green, fire red and lead grey – the term "colourful" takes on a whole new dimension in this impressive thermal area covering 18km^2 south of Rotorua. The name means "holy water". You can explore the amazing spectacle of the *Thermal Wonderland* on three circular tours (30, 40, 75 minutes). The *Lady Knox Geyser* is active daily shortly after 10.15am. Soap powder is added to the geyser, which offers extra entertainment during the short talk. *Daily 8.30am–5pm | NZ$32.50 | 201 Waiotapu Loop Road | waiotapu.co.nz | ▯▯ K7*

23 MOUNT TARAWERA

85km/1 hr 15 mins from Rotorua (car)
Have you always wanted to see an active volcano from inside? Then, join an adventurous day excursion to the crater.

INSIDER TIP
Descend into the crater

The one-hour journey east from Rotorua in the rustic four-wheel drive bus is already thrilling, and then there's the ascent to the edge of the crater. Here, you are rewarded with a phenomenal view. Next, you slide on the solidified lava into the red crater. It's best if you have sturdy hiking boots, so you don't need to constantly empty your socks!

In 1886, Mount Tarawera erupted

Peer into the crater of Mount Tarawera if you dare!

for six hours; 151 people were killed, and the world-famous Pink & White Terraces were showered in ash. The last eruption was in 1981, so hopefully, only your feet should smoulder. Tours with *Kaitiaki Adventures (summer 8.15am and 1.15pm, winter 10am | NZ$185 | tel. 0800 338 736 | kaitiaki. co.nz).* ⫟ K6–7

24 WHAKATANE & WHITE ISLAND
120km/1 hr 30 mins from Rotorua (car)
The top attraction of the town of Whakatane, towards the east of the Bay of Plenty, has long been White Island, a steaming, active volcanic island 50km from the coast that marks the end of the *Taupo Volcanic Zone.* However, the island has been closed to visitors since 19 December 2019,

when 22 people tragically died after the *Whakaari* volcano erupted. Today, the best (and only) way to see the island is on a flight in a propellor plane *(NZ$249 | tel. 07 308 7760 | whiteislandflights.co.nz).* The *Whakaari Experience Room* at Whakatane's *visitor centre (Mon–Fri 8.30am–5.30pm, Sat/Sun 9am–4pm | Quay Street | whakatane.com)* will tell you all you need to know about White Island with a video and an exhibition. The town of Whakatane is not an especially interesting place, but to the east Ohope has an incredible, long surfing beach. ⫟ L6

25 TAURANGA & MOUNT MAUNGANUI
63km/1 hr from Rotorua (car)

Tauranga (pop. 130,000), New Zealand's fifth largest city, is booming with Aucklanders who have turned their backs on the expensive "big smoke". The country's second largest port is here. Although the town itself doesn't have much to offer, the surrounding area is beautiful.

At the *Bay of Plenty*, where Tauranga is located, the sun shines more often and longer than in other part of New Zealand. The conditions are perfect for enjoying the endless white sandy beaches and superb views of the nearby *Mount Maunganui*. You can climb this 230-m-high, extinct volcano *(on foot 1.5 hrs to summit or 1 hr on the lower path)*. You can also surf, play beach volleyball or sip coffee and enjoy the sea view, e.g. in *Deckchair Café (daily 6.30am–3.30pm | 2 Marine Parade | deckchaircafe.co.nz)*. Or you can relax in a saltwater pool: the recently refurbished 🍴 👫 *Mount Hot Pools (Mon–Sat 7am–10pm, Sun 8am–10pm | NZ\$19 | 9 Adams Av. | tel. 07 577 8551 | mounthotpools.co.nz)* offer various pools from 34°C.

There are shops and restaurants on Maunganui Road. The *Mount Social Club* combines retro interiors with organic food *(daily from 8am | 305 Maunganui Road | tel. 07 574 7773 | social-club.co.nz | \$–\$\$)*. The venue is fit to burst during concerts by local musicians such as the Tauranga Jazz Society. *The Mount*, as the Kiwis call it, is usually fully booked at Christmas.
📖 *K6*

INSIDER TIP
Jazz meets the sound of the sea

26 HOBBITON 👫

85km/1 hr 15 mins by Rotorua (car)
If you like hairy feet and don't mind the trip north-west, this pleasant spot in Matamata is ideal. You can walk through the original film set. The "Shire" lives on here: the colourful round doors in front of the Hobbit caves with mini gardens in the middle of a sheep farm. The entire site nestles among green hills. Genuine *Hobbit* and *Lord of the Rings* fans naturally enjoy a beer in the *Green Dragon* by the crackling fireside. *Daily from 9am | NZ\$89 | book in advance | 501 Buckland Road | tel. 07 888 1505 | hobbitontours.com|* 📖 *J6*

27 WAITOMO GLOWWORM CAVES 👫 🍴

140km/1 hr 50 mins from Rotorua (car)
Excellent caving is on offer in the underground Waitomo Caves – and twinkling glow-worms take care of the illumination. New Zealand glow-worms are not cute little creatures, but fairly unromantic, hungry larvae of the fungus gnat that can also turn to cannibalism. The hungrier they are, the more brightly they glow. Certain enzymes – known as luciferases – make the larvae glow. You will find various tours through the three main caves by boat and on foot at *waitomo. com*. The absolute highlight for adrenalin junkies is the four- or seven-hour *Lost World Tour (daily | from NZ\$425 | tel. 0800 924 866 | waitomo.co.nz)*. You abseil 100m into the mystical caves and hike through the labyrinthine cave system, past waterfalls and gigantic stalactites. If you prefer to

avoid the crowds, you can visit the nearby *Footwhistle Cave*, which is smaller and much quieter than the Waitomo Caves. *Cave World (from NZ$64 | 23 Waitomo Village Road | tel. 0800 228 396 | caveworld.co.nz)* offers daily tours here for small groups, including a bush walk, and underground black water rafting.

In the small town of *Waitomo* you will find fresh Asian and European cuisine at the *Huhu Café (Mon–Thu 5-8pm, Fri-Sun from noon | 10 Waitomo Caves Road | tel. 07 878 6674 | huhucafe.co.nz | $$)*. The terrace offers a fabulous view of the green landscape with massive tree-ferns. If you want to stay, stop at the comfortable backpacker hostel *Kiwi Paka (11 rooms | Hotel Access Road | tel. 07 878 3395 | waitomokiwipaka.co.nz | $)*. The location is very quiet, as Waitomo is secluded – apart from the tourism to the caves. That said, there is one special highlight for children: the neighbouring town of *Otorohanga* is home to the 🐧 *Kiwi House (daily 9am–5pm | NZ$24, children over 5 NZ$8 | 20 Alex Telfer Drive | kiwihouse.org.nz)*, a breeding centre for kiwi birds. The place has everything you need: fresh pizzas, dormitories or single rooms and rustic chalets. And for a special experience your children will talk about for years to come, in 🐧 *Woodlyn Park (10 rooms | 1177 Waitomo Valley Road | tel. 07 878 6666 | woodlynpark.co.nz | $$)*, Otorohanga, you can even spend the night in an old airplane, an excursion steamer or in cave dwellings "Hobbit" style. *▢ J6*

TAUPO

(▢ K7) **Lake Taupo is deep, vast and surrounded by Maori legends. The lake is the focus of the panoramic vistas and the open atmosphere of the town of Taupo (pop. 36,200) on its north-eastern shore.**

This region is truly sporting mad. It's not surprising – it's an outdoor paradise with opportunities for cycling and trout fishing, boat tours and excursions to the geothermal parks. The compact city centre also offers excellent shopping facilities. To get your bearings, it's best to park by the lakeside and admire the view over the snow-covered summit of Mount Tongariro. In New Zealand's oldest national park you can enjoy an adventure exploring the active volcanoes: hiking, mountain biking and even skiing.

SIGHTSEEING

CRATERS OF THE MOON

What's smouldering here? Make sure it's not your feet! You should wear sturdy shoes for this thrilling excursion to the geothermal field about 5km north of Taupo. Two wooden walkways lead over 3km across the volcanic moon landscape with bubbling craters and steam fountains in the middle of the lava rubble. *Daily 10am–4pm | NZ$8 | Karapiti Road | cratersofthemoon.co.nz*

HUKA FALLS

Huka means "foam" in Maori, and it's a fitting name. This thunderous

Hobbiton: welcome to Bilbo's home in the Shire

waterfall is five minutes by car from the centre: 220,000 litres per second of the bluest water flow through a narrow ravine before cascading in wild and foaming torrents about 10m deep into the Waikato River. The *lookout* from Loop Road offers a fabulous, elevated perspective. Or you can get sprayed with foam in a jet boat *(NZ$115)* right beneath the falls. *Huka Falls Road | hukafalls.com*

LAKE TAUPO
It is fathomless and has a fiery history: at 186m at its deepest point and covering an area of about 620km^2 – slightly larger than the Isle of Man – Lake Taupo is New Zealand's largest lake. It was formed by a powerful volcanic eruption in about 180 BCE. Explore the lake and the Maori rock carvings in *Mine Bay* 10km southwest of the city – ideally, on a sailing trip lasting two hours 30 minutes with *Sail Fearless (from NZ$49 | Taupo Marina | tel. 02 2189 1847 | sail fearless.co.nz)* – or in a kayak *(tour providers at the lake or on the local i-site).* ⌁ *J–K7*

DIXIE BROWNS
Here, you can dine with a lake view from morning until evening. The large selection ranges from wraps to pizza and hearty steaks if you are very hungry. The dessert counter has already tempted many visitors. *Daily 6am–10pm | 38 Roberts Street | tel. 07 378 8444 | dixiebrowns.co.nz | $–$$*

Get up close to Huka Falls in a jet boat

the Moon Park. More information is available at *greatlaketaupo.com*. Bike hire and pick-ups are organized by *Adventure Shuttles (504 Mapara Road | tel. 02 2547 0399 | adventure shuttles.co.nz)* five minutes away from Taupo.

WAKEBOARDING

You can try wakeboarding and water skiing for experienced skiers at *Taupowake Park (4 hrs from NZ$75 | book in advance| 201 Karetoto Road | tel. 07 378 7666 | taupowakepark. com)*.

WELLNESS

WAIRAKEI TERRACES 🌂

Hot clouds of steam in the heart of the rainforest: The 13 different mineral pools in the Wairakei Valley will

> **INSIDER TIP**
> The source of happiness

have you forgetting your worries in no time. Your cheeks will be pleasantly rosy by the time you emerge from the healing spring water. *Fri–Wed 8.30am–9pm, Thu until 7pm | NZ$25 | State Highway 1 | Wairakei | tel. 07 378 0913 | wairakeiterraces.co.nz*

REPLETE CAFÉ & STORE

This light and spacious café serves a generous breakfast and is a favourite meeting place for locals and tourists. *Daily 8am–4pm | 45 Heuheu Street | replete.co.nz | $$*

SPORT & ACTIVITIES

CYCLING

Around *Lake Taupo* cyclists and mountain bikers are spoilt for choice: from a level cycle ride by the lake to the single trails, or from a one-hour tour to a three-day trail, with a guide or at your own pace. The top trails are the *Huka Falls Way*, *Great Lake Trails* or *Craters of*

AROUND TAUPO

28 ORAKEI KORAKO
35km/30 mins from Taupo (car)

The extremely unusual geothermal *Ruatapu Caves* are the highlight of this thermal park in Hidden Valley. The rest of the geothermal field – with 23 active natural geysers, thermal springs, bubbling mud pools and vast limestone terraces – is also fascinating. Included in the price is the boat tour via a small lake to the caves. *Daily 9am–4pm | NZ$42 | 494 Orakeikorako Road | orakeikorako.co.nz | ⬭ K7*

⊠ TONGARIRO NATIONAL PARK
90km/1 hr 30 mins from Taupo (car)
The entrance is already dramatic: mystical and smouldering volcanoes with snow-topped peaks rise skywards from the vast steppe-land. Thick clouds scud past, their curious shapes constantly changing. The region south of Taupo is in perpetual motion. *Mount Ngauruhoe* erupted 45 times in the 20th century; the last time was in 1975. The 1953 eruption of *Mount Ruapehu* killed 151 people. Other eruptions were less damaging; the most recent in 2007 caused a massive mud slide. The geothermal activity is constantly monitored, and the early-warning system is effective. Nothing is likely to happen if you are skiing or hiking on the 2,000–3,000-m-high, active volcano.

INSIDER TIP
Ski down a volcano

The ★ *Tongariro Alpine Crossing* is among the world's most popular day hikes. It takes between five and eight hours to cross the surreal volcanic landscape with incredible views. Please note: the summit can get crowded ... The weather must be fine

and the guesthouses in the national park organize the shuttle. Alternatively, you can book from Taupo with *Tongariro Expeditions (daily 6.30, 7.30 and 8.30am | NZ$35, one way | tel. 0800 828 763 | tongariroexpeditions. com).*

The *Taranaki Falls Walk* is a shorter alternative or more suitable in bad weather. It's a simple, two-hour circular tour of the volcanic landscape with views of Mount Ruapehu and a waterfall. Hiking tours to the edge of the crater with *(tel. 0800 429 255 | tongariroguidedwalks.nz)* or without a guide are *tremendous!*

The Maori chief Te Heuheu gave the park to the people of New Zealand in 1887; about 100 years later UNESCO designated Tongariro National Park both as a UNESCO World Cultural Site and World Natural Heritage Site. *Tongariro National Park Visitor Centre (daily 8am–5pm, in winter 8am–4.30pm | free admission | SH48 | doc. govt.nz)* in Whakapapa Village is a treasure trove of information about Maori myths, nature and volcanoes as well as the starting point for many hikes.

In winter, you can choose from two skiing areas: *Mount Ruapehu* in Whakapapa or slightly further south *Turoa*. The ski lifts also run in summer – for hiking enthusiasts who want to save time. Shopping and additional accommodation are available in the *national park (crossroads SH4 and 47). ⬭ J8*

GISBORNE

(◻ M7) **Rise and shine! In Gisborne, you can watch the famous sunrise – this is the first city in the world to see daylight! The town has a proud history – in the 14th century, some of the first Maoris arrived on land here. Captain Cook also first came to New Zealand here in 1769.**

"Gizzy", as the 36,000 inhabitants call their town, is located in lucrative Poverty Bay, where there is plenty of sunshine, the vines grow well and the orchards produce delicious fruit.

Only the hapless Captain Cook called it "Poverty Bay" because when he set foot on land, there was a skirmish with the Maoris, so the crew had to leave again without any new supplies.

Gisborne is situated in the eastern part of North Island, at the foot of the spectacular East Cape, which is surrounded by Maori settlements, picturesque bays and empty surf beaches. Northwest of the city, inland between the Bay of Plenty and Hawke's Bay, is the giant nature park

Mount Ruapehu in Tongariro National Park – or Mount Doom from *The Lord of the Rings*?

Te Urewera with its lakes and unspoilt forests. On the way south, the wine region Hawke's Bay is linked to the wonderful Mahia Peninsula.

SIGHTSEEING

CAPTAIN COOK STATUE

The British mariner follows you here at every turn – the attractive 1-km-long *River Walkway (starting at Waikanae Beach)* along the Turanganui and Taruheru rivers leads past the great explorer.

KAITHI HILL

At the viewpoint on Gisborne's mountain, also called Titirangi Hill, you will find another Captain Cook statue, which is the joke of the entire town. Firstly, it bears little resemblance to Cook, and secondly his uniform is Italian. But the views are impressive and at the summit there are lovely, shady walking routes in the lush *Titirangi Domain*. This was once the site of a Maori Pa – a fortified village. You can either make the ascent along Queens Drive or else walk up the mountain *(1–2 hrs return trip).*

EATING & DRINKING

EASTEND CAFÉ

Small, inconspicuous café with surprisingly good food and excellent coffee. The most popular dish with regulars is eggs benedict! *Tue–Sat 8am–3pm | 250 Marine Parade | tel. 06 838 6070 | $*

THE WHARF BAR & GRILL

Cultivated atmosphere located in the Inner Harbour where the wine instantly tastes even better with a view of the great yachts. Versatile menu, breakfast also served at weekends. *Tue–Fri 11am–9pm, Sat 9am–9pm, Sun 9am–3pm | 60 The Esplanade | tel. 06 281 0035 | wharfbar.co.nz | $$*

SPORT & ACTIVITIES

SURFING

You'll always find surf here somewhere. It's not surprising that some of New Zealand's best surfers come from

How many people can fish from the 600-m pier in Tolaga Bay?

Gisborne. The pros at *New Wave NZ* have surf boards for hire and give lessons *(Tue–Fri 9am–5pm, Sat until 1pm, Sun 10am–2pm | 189 Awapuni Road | tel. 06 867 1439 | newwavenz. com)*.

BEACHES

The city beach *Waikanae* is long and its location at sunrise is very practical. But around the East Cape you will find much more attractive beaches such as ✱ *Makorori Beach*. This legendary surf beach only 10km from Gisborne's city centre is also perfect for bathing: a golden sandy beach with rock pools.

WELLNESS

MORERE HOT SPRINGS 🐷

Sadly, more and more hot pools in New Zealand are charging extortionate prices for a dip in the hot spring water. Luckily, the Morere Hot Springs with hot salt water are still affordable. They might not be elaborate in design, but are stunning in their location – a forest full of nīkau palm trees. Entry is just NZ$14, a private pool just NZ$4 more. *Daily 10am–5.15pm | 3968 State Highway 2 | tel. 06 837 8856 | FB: Morere Hot Springs*

AROUND GISBORNE

🔟 RERE ROCKSLIDE
50km/45 mins from Gisborne (car)

If you love waterslides, north-west of Gisborne you will find your paradise: you can slide for 70m on the natural rockslide into a natural rock pool. If

INSIDER TIP
The rockslide of your dreams

you find the rocks on the slide uncomfortable, a boogie board or air mattress is recommended. The most applause goes to people who slide backwards. *Public access | Wharekopae Road | Ngatapa | 🗺 L7*

🔟 TE UREWERA
160km/2 hrs 20 mins from Gisborne to Aniwaniwa (car)

This secluded, enchanting fairy-tale forest has a giant lake, waterfalls and impressive mountain ranges where you can easily get lost. It's advisable to keep to the well-established hiking paths. They start in *Aniwaniwa*.

Since 2014, the largest native forestland in all New Zealand is in the hands of the Tuhoi, a powerful Maori tribe from this region, whose members also call themselves "Children of the Mist". Early in the morning, when the mists rise over the impressive *Lake Waikaremoana*, you will also understand why. From Aniwaniwa you can go on day tours or a three- to four-day (hilly!) *Great Walk* around the lake with fantastic views. There are 40 Department of Nature Conservation (DOC) huts in the park that you can book in advance at *doc. govt.nz.* ⌑ *K–L7*

32 TOLAGA BAY

55km/45 mins from Gisborne (car)
This small coastal town has a pier that extends over 600m into the sea in front of a superb backdrop of white cliffs, beach and estuary. It a popular location for photos, and a favorite spot for anglers. ⌑ *M7*

33 EAST CAPE LIGHTHOUSE ★

190km/3 hrs from Gisborne (car)
A lighthouse of superlatives – this is New Zealand's easternmost point. After that, it's out into the Pacific. The East Cape is one of the first places in the world to experience the sunrise. Early-morning sport is also included – the ascent to the lighthouse involves 750 steps, which is exhausting, but the magnificent view along the green coast is really worth the effort. You

cannot climb the 15-m-high tower itself.

You should allow plenty of time for the drive from Gisborne; on your way you'll pass one fantastic beach after the next! It would be a pity not to explore them. If you want to stay overnight at East Cape, it's best to head for *Tokomaru Bay* or *Hick's Bay*. *Lottin Point*, a 40-minute drive from the lighthouse, is widely regarded as one of the best fishing spots in the country. ⌑ *M6*

INSIDER TIP
Top-notch sea fishing

34 MAHIA PENINSULA

105km/1 hr 15 mins from Gisborne (car)
Another genuine insider tip in Hawke's Bay is Mahia Peninsula – it's off the beaten track and surrounded by dream beaches with crystal-clear water. You can explore the adventurous, gravel, coastal route Kinikini Road past steep cliffs, green valleys and the view over the peninsula to the mainland. The panoramic view from *Mokotahi Hill* (20 minutes uphill) is fantastic – the white rocky headland is a distinctive landmark of the peninsula. *Mahia Beach Motel & Holiday Park (43 Moana Drive)* on the beach at Hawke's Bay has a small café called *Funky Fish*. ⌑ *L–M8*

35 NAPIER ★

215km/3 hrs from Gisborne (car)
Wine, cycle routes and architecture – the art deco town of Napier (pop. 61,000) on Hawke's Bay – at first sight rather unremarkable – has plenty to offer. After the disastrous earthquake,

which destroyed the bay in 1931 and killed 256 people, the city was rebuilt in three years with a typical "can-do" attitude. The 147 art deco buildings that were distributed across the city now count among the best preserved of their kind. You can download the Art Deco Napier App (artdeconapier.com | ⏱ 2 hrs) and tick off all the buildings as you explore the city and beautiful wharf with a view of the distant Cape Kidnappers on foot or by bicycle. Vintage Car Tours (hooters-hire. co.nz) offers the chance to explore the city in an old Buick. Stock up on vintage clothing at retro boutiques Charleston Chic and Decorum and dress the part. The whole town joins in the fun and dresses in the style of the Roaring Twenties for Art Deco Weekend in February.

INSIDER TIP
Travel back to the Roaring Twenties

In Havelock North (⅏ K8), which is 20km away, is the first-class wine estate Craggy Range Vineyard (253 Waimarama Road | craggyrange.com | $$$), with a newly refurbished restaurant – next to Te Mata Peak, which also offers a fabulous view of the surrounding valley and bay.

A further 20km southeastwards and you can admire the aerial acrobatics of northern gannets at Cape Kidnappers (⅏ L8). At low tide you can tackle the 10-km-long beach hike to the nesting sites of the gannet colony, or take a tractor ride with Gannet Beach Adventures (from NZ$55 | gannets.com). The birds' nesting season is from November to February. ⅏ K–L8

WHANGANUI NATIONAL PARK

(⅏ H–J8) **Although Whanganui is a quiet town (pop. 40,000) with few attractions, it is built alongside New Zealand's longest river (290km), the Whanganui, that crosses vast swathes of ★ Whanganui National Park.**

That said, you should still take a look at the beautiful St Paul's Memorial Church (20 Anaua Street) filled with Maori art before you disappear into the lush vegetation of the national park. For this you have several options: you can either travel on the 1899 paddle steamer, the Waimarie (daily 11am, 2pm, approx. 2 hrs | approx. NZ$49 | waimarie.co.nz), which departs from Taupo Quay in the city centre; by car along Whanganui River Road; or gently by canoe or kayak.

SIGHTSEEING

WHANGANUI RIVER ROAD

Welcome to the middle of nowhere! As soon as you are swallowed up by the rainforest of Whanganui National Park (shortly after Raetihi at SH4), you lose all connection with the present – you are likely only to meet the odd car travelling towards you on the winding road. Switch off the car engine now and then to listen to the loud crackling of the insects in the bush. From

Vintage cars don't look out of place on the art deco streets of Napier

Pipiriki (25km from Raetihi) the road winds 79km to Whanganui directly along the river, past Maori meeting houses with artfully carved façades and plenty of viewpoints above the Whanganui River. Then, suddenly, in the middle of the luscious greenery, you'll come across the old Catholic mission 🎋 🐖 *Jerusalem (20 beds/ 1 double room | from NZ$30 per person | tel. 06 342 8190 | compassion. org.nz)*. Cows graze in front of the yellow-red timber church and ferns overgrow the statues of Mary in the garden. It's easy to see how the nuns made their peace with the outside world in this fairy-tale location. You can stay overnight either in a dormitory with bunk beds or a double room with bathroom. *Jerusalem Daybook* is the perfect night-time reading; it was written by New Zealand's most famous poet James K. Baxter who in the 1960s lived in a hippie commune on the Whanganui River. Fill the car with petrol before the tour and pack plenty of supplies! 🗺 *J8*

EATING & DRINKING

THE YELLOW HOUSE

A yellow painted wooden villa with a beautiful garden filled with plants near the Whanganui River. Varied all-day breakfast menu with quinoa porridge, eggs benedict or buttermilk pancakes. For lunch there are burgers, pasta and fish & chips. *Mon–Fri 8am–4pm, Sat/Sun from 8.30am | 17 Pitt Street | tel. 06 345 0083 | yellowhousecafe.co.nz | $*

Enjoy a canoe tour along the magical Whanganui River

SPORT & ACTIVITIES

WHANGANUI JOURNEY

That's the name of one of New Zealand's Great Walks that is actually a canoe tour. The tour takes three to five days and includes the dense bush of *Taumarunui (▥ J7) (about 160km north of Whanganui)* to Pipiriki and is worth completing in shorter sections. *Taumarunui Canoe Hire (from NZ$70 | 292 Hikumutu Road | tel. 07 895 7483 | taumarunuicanoehire.co.nz)*, with its own freedom campsite, hires out canoes, reserves huts and campsites along the route and picks you up again at the end.

AROUND WHANGANUI

☒ FORGOTTEN WORLD HIGHWAY

120km/1 hr 30 mins from Whanganui to the starting point of Stratford (car)
Make sure that this road is not

$–$$) the host even stamps your passport. Because there is very little traffic on the highway, you can drive slowly in the especially beautiful spots – e.g. along the Tangarakau River, which flows through lush vegetation between high cliff faces. That's what the world must have looked like when dinosaurs still existed! *H8–J7*

☷ MOUNT TARANAKI/EGMONT NATIONAL PARK

140km/2 hrs from Whanganui (car)
At 2,518m, *Mount Taranaki* (also known as Mount Egmont) is twice as high as Vesuvius. Although it has not erupted for over 300 years, it is an extremely temperamental volcano and, near the summit, the weather can change within minutes. However, tours of the lower slopes are easy to undertake. The 80-minute *Wilkies Pools Loop Track* starts above the *Dawson Falls Visitor Centre (Manaia Road | tel. 02 7443 0248 | doc.govt.nz)* in *Egmont National Park*, which surrounds the mountain. It continues through fairy-tale forests full of moss-covered trees to Kapuni River, where you can swim in the fossilized lava pools with a view of Mount Taranaki. The best place for photos of the volcano is the viewing platform at the *Egmont National Park Visitor Centre (2879 Egmont Road | doc.govt. nz)*. Between June and October you can also race down the volcano on skis and snowboards. About 1,500m below the edge of the crater is *Manganui (skitaranaki.co.nz)*, a small *skiing region* with several drag lifts. *H8*

forgotten by the world! The *State Highway 43* between Stratford and Taumarunui is far too beautiful for that. The highway runs for 150km through a fantasy landscape with green hills, ravines and waterfalls and past deserted coal mines as far as New Zealand's only republic to have been governed by a poodle: *Whangamomona*. You don't believe it? Then, stop and ask one of the 170 residents. In the *Whangamomona Hotel (6018 Ohura Road | tel. 06 762 5823 | whangamomonahotel.co.nz |*

88 SURF HIGHWAY (SH 45)

90km/1 hr 10 mins from Whanganui to the starting point of Hawera (car)

On one side is the Tasman Sea and on the other side is the volcanic Mount Taranaki with its snow-covered summit: along the Surf Highway 45 between New Plymouth and Hawera (105km), you will not be able to stop admiring the beautiful scenery. The following stops are worthwhile: *Oakura*, because of the many artists and surfers and the *Arts Trail (oakuraarts.co.nz)* with galleries and art workshops; *Kumera Patch*, where you get the best surf waves; *Komene Road*, because here beginners can also stay on a surfboard. 🞝 *G–H 7–8*

89 NEW PLYMOUTH

160km/2 hrs from Whanganui (car)

The city (pop. 56,000) on the Tasman Sea is secluded but still in touch with the times: the *Govett Brewster Art Gallery (daily 10am–5pm | NZ$15 | 42 Queen Street | govettbrewster.com)*, with its futuristic mirror façade, is considered one of the top venues for contemporary art in New Zealand. The interactive 🞝 *Puke Ariki Museum (Mon–Fri 10am–6pm, Sat/Sun to 5pm | free admission | 1 Ariki Street | pukeariki.com | ⏱ 1 hr)* provides an engaging insight into Maori culture and the history of the region. The city also stands out from the rest thanks to first-class restaurants, such as *Social Kitchen (40 Powderham Street | tel. 06 757 2711 | social-kitchen.co.nz | $$)*, the 7km-long *Coastal Walkway* at *Fitzroy Surf Beach*, and one of New Zealand's best botanical gardens. The 52-hectare *Pukekura Park (10 Fillis Street)* is an enchanting city oasis with tall trees, lakes, waterfalls and rowing boats. 🞝 *H7*

WHERE TO START?

Waterfront: Leave your car on the waterfront and you're right in the centre. In the city everything is close by and many attractions like the Te Papa National Museum and fabulous restaurants are at the harbour. From here, you can take a stroll down Cuba Street to visit the art galleries or admire the graffiti art that adorns many of the houses there.

WELLINGTON

(🞝 H10) **"Windy" Wellington is one of the world's stormiest cities. The New Zealand capital (pop. 210,000), at the southern end of North Island, is on the famous Cook Strait that is like a wind tunnel between North and South Island.**

But you don't need to worry about constant bad weather here, because Wellington offers compact sightseeing with museums, parliament, parks and a definite feel-good factor. What's more, the restaurants are excellent – and all this is in a beautiful seaside location (the *Sculpture Trail* on the waterfront offers a walk past works by New Zealand artists).

As a capital city, Wellington is fairly relaxed. City life is a successful

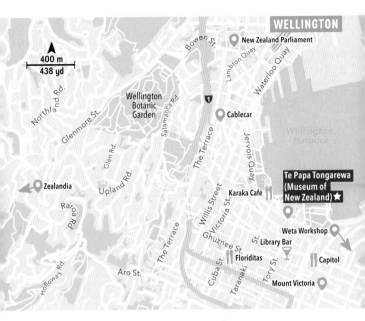

400 m
438 yd

New Zealand Parliament

Wellington Botanic Garden

Cablecar

Zealandia

Wellington Harbour

Te Papa Tongarewa (Museum of New Zealand) ★

Karaka Café

Weta Workshop

Library Bar

Floriditas

Capitol

Mount Victoria

mixture of the artistic and alternative set on *Cuba Street* and people in smart suits at *Lambton Quay*, the main shopping street, with the New Zealand parliament located at the end. Here, at least, you get the feeling of being in a metropolis. Perhaps, the relaxed atmosphere is explained by the city's location – on a geological powder keg. Wellington is close to the Wairarapa Fault and is one the most exposed cities to earthquakes in New Zealand – this is impressively recorded on *wellingtonquakelive.co.nz*.

SIGHTSEEING

TE PAPA TONGAREWA (MUSEUM OF NEW ZEALAND) ★ 👥 🐗

The Te Reo Maori name for this ultra-modern museum, effectively New Zealand's National Museum, means "place of treasures". Here, there are manifold treasures: masks that illustrate the meaning of the *moko*, the Maoris' traditional face tattoos, dinosaur teeth and animal products, sculptures made from feathers, photos from the nation's founding era, works by contemporary artists, and so on. It is very entertaining and some of the exhibits are interactive. The specialist areas at Te Papa are exhibitions about nature and Polynesian history, Maori culture and the country's geology. The exhibition about World War I, *Gallipoli*, is exceptional and was created by the director of *The Hobbit*, Peter Jackson, with the *Weta Workshop Studios*. There is an attractive shop and pleasant cafés. Plan at least two hours or more for

Ride the cable car for a panoramic view of Wellington

1 hr) – you can even admire the earthquake shock absorbers in the basement – when everything moves, at least parliament should stay standing. *Molesworth Street*

CABLE CAR

The small, red cable car transports you from Lambton Quay, 122m high, to the district of Kelburn. If you want to enjoy some background to the views over the city and harbour, you should visit the small *museum (daily 10am–5pm | free admission)* and learn about the history of the cable car. Alternatively, you can explore the galaxies above Wellington in *Space Place (Tue, Fri, Sat 10am–11pm, Mon, Wed, Thu, Sun 10am–5pm | NZ$14 | museumswellington.org.nz/ space-place).* The descent back to the city passes through the attractive *Botanic Gardens* with dense vegetation and native and exotic plants. *Mon–Wed 7.30am–8pm, Thu, Fri 7.30am–9pm, Sat 8.30am–9pm, Sun 8.30am–8pm, every 10 mins | NZ$5/ single trip | wellingtoncablecar.co.nz*

your visit. *Daily 10am–6pm | free admission | 55 Cable Street | tepapa. govt.nz |* 2–3 hrs

NEW ZEALAND PARLIAMENT

Beehive is the popular name for the 70-m-high, round concrete building where the ministries (naturally...) work diligently. The Beehive is connected to the *Parliament Buildings* and the *Parliamentary Library*. In the parliamentary chamber (as in Westminster) visitors can observe the public debates. The 120 Members of Parliament make decisions here about Aotearoa's wellbeing; seven of them are representatives of the Maoris. The free guided tour of the parliament and library building is interesting *(daily 10am–4pm every half hour | reservation tel. 04 817 9503 | parliament.nz |*

ZEALANDIA

Kiwis, takahe and tuataras only five minutes from the centre of Wellington: this nature reserve with traditional vegetation at the heart of the city is unique in the world. On 30km of trails you can discover rare native birds, reptiles and creatures like the weta – the scary giant insect that looks like a cricket and rose to fame when Weta Workshop Studios (see below) were named after it. The tour *Zealandia by Night* starts at sunset and lasts two hours 30 minutes. With an expert guide, it is enthralling and, if you're lucky, you will see or hear a kiwi (the bird is active at night). Wrap up warm, even in summer! *Daily 9am–5pm | NZ$23, Night Tour NZ$85 | Waiapu Road | visitzealandia.com*

MOUNT VICTORIA

From the local mountain at a height of 196m, you have a fabulous panoramic view over the region around Wellington, the harbour as far as Lower Hutt, Cook Straight and the (earth- quake-proof) wooden houses on the slopes. Hiking and mountain-bike trails wind their way up and down Mount Victoria to offer constantly changing and magnificent views. *Above Oriental Parade*

WETA WORKSHOP STUDIOS 👫 ⅀

Life-size models and original props from films like *The Hobbit*, *King Kong* or *Lord of the Rings*. During a 45-minute tour of the Oscar-winning studio for special effects and costume design in Wellington (also in Auckland), kids and adults get a great visual show of how to animate fantasy characters on the computer. *Adults NZ$49, children NZ$25, book tickets online in advance | Weka Street/corner of Camperdown Road | www.weta workshop.com*

EATING & DRINKING

Wellington boasts some of the country's finest restaurants. On *Cuba Street* there are cheap eateries, whereas the smarter restaurants on the *Waterfront* are pricier. There's no such thing as bad coffee in the city that invented the flat white. Countless cafés in Wellington compete for the title of "best coffee in town". 2021's top five were *Havana, Peoples Coffee, Coffee Supreme, Raglan Roast and Café L'Affarre*. If the weather's not up to much, why not hop from one coffee shop to the next?

INSIDER TIP
Café hopping on a rainy day

CAPITOL

Chef Tom Hutchinson does away with the frills for fuss-free Italian-influenced dining that's all about taste. His secret: he only uses choice ingredients from the region that are in season. Fresh mussels, lamb and fish are served up with risotto, focaccia or gnocchi. *Wed–Sun 5–11pm | 10 Kent Terrace | tel. 04 384 2855 | capitolrestaurant.co.nz | $$*

FLORIDITAS

A light, modern restaurant on Cuba Street, where every guest is greeted like an old friend. Fantastic food with exceptional dishes like swordfish on risotto or grilled duck. The desserts are good enough to lick off the plate! *Mon–Sat 7am–10pm | 161 Cuba Street | bookings@floriditas.co.nz | floriditas.co.nz | $$–$$$*

KARAKA CAFÉ

Everything is Kiwi in this harbour restaurant: the music, decor and food – hearty *hangi*, tender lamb and fresh mussels, which are served with wine or beer made in Aotearoa. You can enjoy the drinks outside in the sun on the comfy bean bags if you wish. *Daily breakfast & lunch, Fri/Sat also dinner | 2 Taranaki Street | tel. 04 916 8369 | karakacafe.co.nz | $–$$*

SHOPPING

You'll find fashion, high-tech and sports shops at *Lambton Quay*, alternative art and knick-knacks on *Cuba Street* at *Iko Iko (118 Cuba Mall | ikoiko. co.nz)* or *Cosmic (97 Cuba Street | cosmicnz.co.nz)*. Authentic Maori artwork is available at the *Ora Gallery (23 Allen Street | ora.co.nz)* or *Maori Arts Gallery (1 Boatshed | Frank Kitts Park | maori-arts-gallery.myshopify.com)*.

BEACHES

Wellington's best beaches are on *Island Bay*, *Oriental Parade* (close to the city) and *Lyall Bay*, with views of South Island.

NIGHTLIFE

Wellingtonians are good at partying. Most pubs and bars are at the *Harbour* or *Courtenay Place*.

LIBRARY BAR

If you run out of things to chat about, here's some inspiration. The quaint pub with tapas menu is packed full of old books. A quirky ambiance with interesting avant-garde cocktails. *Mon–Thu from 5pm, Fri–Sun from 4pm | 53 Courtenay Place | thelibrary. co.nz*

FERRIES

In stormy weather the ferry crossing to

With a bit of luck, you may spot a rare kaka on Kapiti Island

South Island can be a bit choppy; in fine weather it's wonderfully relaxing. The *Interislander ferry (Aotea Quay, approx. 2km from the centre | tel. 0800 802 802, 04 498 3302 | greatjourneysofnz.co.nz/interislander)* departs five times daily and takes about three hours to get to South Island. The competition *Bluebridge (tel. 0800 844 844 | 04 471 6188 | bluebridge.co.nz)* departs four times a day from opposite the main station at Waterloo Quay. Pre-book car ferries in high season. It's worth comparing the two ferry operators.

AROUND WELLINGTON

🟦 KAPITI COAST
45km/40 mins from Wellington (car)
North of Wellington, you reach 40-km wild beaches with small, charming towns surrounded by forests and mountains – the Kapiti Coast. A ferry ride away is *Kapiti Island*, a nature reserve with numerous rare birds such as the kiwi, kaka and the beautiful saddleback. The sea surrounding the island is also a reserve and if you're lucky you'll see dolphins during the crossing.

Two hiking trails lead to the 520-m-high *Tuteremoana*, the rocky coast is particularly spectacular on the western side. Visits to the island are restricted – you need permission from the *Department of Conservation (DOC; wellingtonvc@doc.govt.nz)*; you can apply in advance by email. You should also organize in advance the boat trip with the *Kapiti Island Eco Experience (approx. NZ$85 | tel. 0800 433 779 | kapitiislandeco.co.nz)* or *Kapiti Island Nature Tours (approx. NZ$82 | tel. 0800 527 484 | kapitiisland.com)* from Paraparaumu. Otherwise, book the full programme including nature guide from *Kapiti Island Nature Tours (approx. NZ$185)*.

In *Queen Elizabeth Park* just behind Paekakariki on the Kapiti Coast, you can explore the endless sand dunes, surf, enjoy fabulous hiking tours or horse riding with *Kapiti Stables (tel. 02 7355 3046)*. 📱 H–J10

🟦 MARTINBOROUGH
80km/1 hr 15 mins from Wellington (car)
The pleasant town with charming old buildings surrounded by meadows and vineyards is in the wine-growing region of *Wairarapa* – in the vicinity of some of New Zealand's most famous vineyards such as *Ata Rangi (atarangi.co.nz)* or *Palliser (palliser.co.nz)*. Cycle tours to the vineyards *(greenjersey.co.nz)* or a wine tour from Wellington *(flatearth.co.nz)* guarantee that you can also taste a fine drop.

At *Cape Palliser* (📱 J11) an attractive lighthouse surveys the southernmost tip of North Island *(1 hr from Martinborough)* with lazy fur seals on the rocks. The wild coastline offers countless photo opportunities. 📱 J10

SOUTH ISLAND

FILM TERRAIN

There is plenty of space on South Island because just a fifth of all New Zealanders, or 1.1 million people, live here. But the South has one million more sheep than North Island!

The emptiness of the countryside makes it an ideal filming location; scouts can choose between rainforests, mountains, glaciers, rivers, beaches, lakes and old gold-digger towns. The landscapes are as different as the weather. It's not unusual to experience four seasons in a day, which explains the oft-seen down jacket-shorts-sandals combo.

The other-worldly Lake Erskine in Fiordland National Park

In what ways does South Island surpass North Island? There are fewer traffic jams (there are hardly any big cities) and definitely more lumberjack competitions (you have to pass the time somehow!). There are more national parks (nine out of a total of 14), the biggest ski areas, the best oysters, more hours of sunshine in the summer, but unfortunately also more Antarctic winds. In short: on South Island Mother Earth plays the main role and you're just an extra – against the backdrop of Nature's magnificent spectacle.

SOUTH ISLAND

MARCO POLO HIGHLIGHTS

★ **MARLBOROUGH SOUNDS**
Labyrinthine fjord landscape with jade-green water and lodgings in the ancient rainforest ➤ p. 91

★ **KAIKOURA**
Spot sperm whales and try freshly caught langoustine ➤ p. 98

★ **CATLINS**
Magnificent nature with seals, penguins and hardly any tourists ➤ p. 106

★ **STEWART ISLAND**
Watch kiwis and take photos of the flaming red sunsets ➤ p. 106

★ **MILFORD SOUND**
Photogenic fjord with rugged cliffs and waterfalls ➤ p. 112

Franz-Josef-Gletscher ★

Franz Josef
p. 122

Gillespies Beach 26
Lake Matheson 25 24
Aoraki/Mount Cook ★
Lake Paringa 27 p. 121

Tasman Glacier Lake Cruise ★

Lake Ohau 22
21 Mount Aspiring National Park
19 Lake Wanaka
8
Wānaka

17 **Milford Sound ★**
Glenorchy 20
18 Arrowtown
Queenstown ★
p. 114

315km, 4 hrs

Doubtful Sound 16
Te Anau
p. 111

643km, 8 hrs 25 mins

213km, 2 hrs 40 mins

SOUTHLAND

OTAGO

Gore
Milton
Winton
Mataura
Balclutha
Riverton 15
14 Invercargill
12 **Catlins ★**
13 Bluff

Stewart Island ★
p. 106
Bathing Beach

100 km
62.14 mi

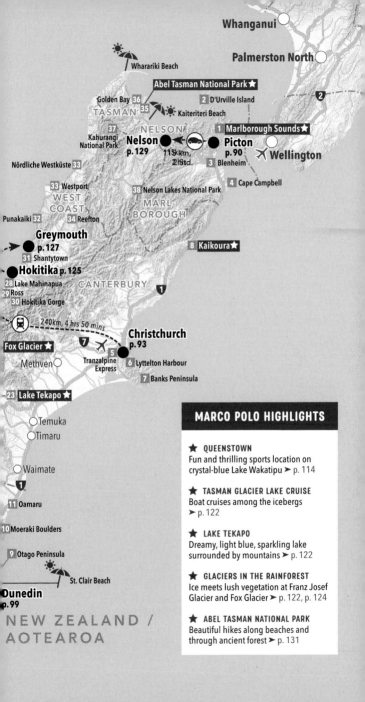

Whanganui

Palmerston North

Whariki Beach

Abel Tasman National Park ★

Golden Bay **36**
TASMAN **35** ★ Kaiteriteri Beach

2 D'Urville Island

NELSON

37
Kahurangi
National Park
Nelson
p. 129

1 Marlborough Sounds ★

Picton
p. 90

115 km,
2 hrs std.

Wellington

Nördliche Westküste **33**

3 Blenheim

4 Cape Campbell

33 Westport
WEST
COAST

38 Nelson Lakes National Park

MARL-
BOROUGH

Punakaiki **32**   **34** Reefton

Greymouth
p. 127

31 Shantytown

8 Kaikoura ★

Hokitika p. 125

28 Lake Mahinapua
29 Ross
CANTERBURY
30 Hokitika Gorge

240km, 4 hrs 50 mins

Christchurch
p. 93

Fox Glacier ★

Methven

7

Tranzalpine
Express

5
6 Lyttelton Harbour

7 Banks Peninsula

23 Lake Tekapo ★

Temuka
Timaru

Waimate

11 Oamaru

10 Moeraki Boulders

9 Otago Peninsula

St. Clair Beach

Dunedin
p. 99

NEW ZEALAND /
AOTEAROA

MARCO POLO HIGHLIGHTS

★ **QUEENSTOWN**
Fun and thrilling sports location on
crystal-blue Lake Wakatipu ➤ p. 114

★ **TASMAN GLACIER LAKE CRUISE**
Boat cruises among the icebergs
➤ p. 122

★ **LAKE TEKAPO**
Dreamy, light blue, sparkling lake
surrounded by mountains ➤ p. 122

★ **GLACIERS IN THE RAINFOREST**
Ice meets lush vegetation at Franz Josef
Glacier and Fox Glacier ➤ p. 122, p. 124

★ **ABEL TASMAN NATIONAL PARK**
Beautiful hikes along beaches and
through ancient forest ➤ p. 131

PICTON

(□ H10) **Every time a ferry arrives from North Island, this small town (pop. 3,000) on Queen Charlotte Sound comes to life. That's when restaurants and cafés on the waterfront fill up and tour operators organizing trips to Marlborough Sounds get busy.**

The glistening green water and beautiful historic buildings invite you to stay a night and taste the fresh fish in the numerous excellent restaurants. Directly from the harbour you can hike the Tirohanga Track (45 minutes) to a viewpoint with a fabulous vista over the Sounds. And if you want to travel further, *Queen Charlotte Drive* heads from Picton on a winding road for 40km past tranquil bays to Havelock. You should definitely stop at the *Cullens Point lookout* to photograph the fjord!

EATING & DRINKING

LE CAFÉ

Enjoy lamb and fish dishes with views of the gleaming green of Queen Charlotte Sound. They use organic ingredients that are locally grown and there's tasty beer and regular live music. *Daily 7am–midnight | 12–14 London Quay | tel. 03 573 5588 | lecafepicton.co.nz | $*

SPORT & ACTIVITIES

BOAT TOURS

What about a kayak tour through the tranquil water of Queen Charlotte Sound? A half-day tour with the *Marlborough Sounds Adventure Company (tel. 03 573 6078 | marlboroughsounds.co.nz)* costs approx. NZ$105. Or would you prefer a *Gourmet Cruise (NZ$120 | tel. 0800 504 090 | cougarline.co.nz)* to *Furneaux Lodge* (green-lipped mussels!) in the dense vegetation of *Endeavour Inlet*? Both are great!

DOLPHIN CRUISE 👯

Swimming with dolphins is particularly safe in the calm waters of the Marlborough Sounds. But it's also good to watch the jumping bottlenose and Hector's dolphins from the boat (children under eight are not allowed in the water). *E-Ko Tours* start in Picton *(adults NZ$99, children over five years NZ$55; boat tour + swimming with dolphins: adults NZ$165, children NZ$135 | 1 Wellington Street | tel. 03 573 8040 | e-ko.nz).*

HIKING

The popular *Queen Charlotte Track* winds 70km through the bush and over mountains with views of jade-green fjords. From Picton you can join a *one-day guided walk* with *Wilderness Guides (NZ$365 | tel. 03 573 5432 | wildernessguidesnz.com).*

SAILING

On the *Steadfast*, a reconstruction of a 1913 French cutter, you can glide silently

INSIDER TIP
Cast off for the past

through Queen Charlotte Sound. *3 hrs | adults NZ$95, children NZ$55 incl. food | tel. 03 576 5298 | steadfastsail.co.nz*

Life in Picton runs according to the ferry schedule

AROUND PICTON

■ MARLBOROUGH SOUNDS ★

50km/1 hr 5 mins from Picton to Cowshed Bay (car)

"Fifty Shades of Green": the clear water gleams like polished jade and the shore is covered with the dark green rainforest. Houses stand boldly on rock spurs in the chirping greenery and on the shore there are scores of small hidden bays. Twenty per cent of New Zealand's coastline is in Marlborough Sounds – there's so much to discover in this landscape of fjords, which, according to Maori legend, was raised by the tentacles of a giant octopus. There are flooded valleys where dolphins swim and green-lipped mussels grow. If you are camping or caravanning, e.g. along the *Kenepuru Sound*, there are plenty of small beaches for camping. *Cowshed Bay*, *Nikau Cove* and *Picnic Bay* are particularly attractive. This is a place where you can forget time – for example at *Nydia Bay Lodge (24 beds | tel. 03 579 8411 | onthetracklodge.nz | $$)*, where you can sleep in wooden chalets, Mongolian yurts or in an old train carriage. It's best to be dropped off here by the ⚑ *Pelorus Sound Mailboat (1.5 hrs from Havelock | tel. 03 574 1088 | themailboat.co.nz)* and spend several days kayaking, snorkelling and hiking along the *Nydia Track*, miles away from any roads. 🕮 *G–H10*

The dark fur seals against the white rocks of Cape Campbell make for a great photo

☑ D'URVILLE ISLAND

90km/1hr 50 mins from Picton on gravel road to Okiwi Bay (car), then 1 hr to French Pass and 15 mins by ferry

It doesn't get more remote: only 52 people live on D'Urville Island, which is bigger than the island of Jersey. Arriving here, at the northern end of Marlborough Sounds, is an adventure in itself; but it's worth it. From Okiwi Bay, it's about an hour's drive on a gravel road with a film-set vista over the green cliffs and sea. At the end of the road is the French Pass, where the tides regularly form giant whirlpools in the sea. You can take a small car ferry from here *(tel. 03 576 5330 | durvillecrossings.co.nz)* to the other side. The few fishermen and nature conservationists, who live on D'Urville Island, will be delighted to see you and keen to tell you where you can fish for the best blue cod and snapper, and which are the most worthwhile hikes through the wilderness. In the *Wilderness Resort (6 rooms | Rural Bag 1211 Rai Valley | tel. 03 576 5268 | durvilleisland.co.nz | $$)* you can stay overnight in wooden huts on the beach. Driftwood Eco Tours *(driftwood ecotours.co.nz)* offers multi-day trips incl. the journey here. 🕮 *G–H10*

3 BLENHEIM
30km/25 mins from Picton (car)

Even if you're not into wine and have never wanted to become a connoisseur, there's a good chance that you will soon be sniffing fine vintages if you come to Blenheim. The area around the small town is New Zealand's principal wine-growing region *Marlborough* (75 % of all NZ wines come from here). The region's prize-winning Sauvignon Blancs are excellent. Try a glass of *Cloudy Bay* on the beach in *Cloudy Bay* or treat yourself to some wines from the *Hans Herzog* winery *(81 Jeffries Road | herzog.co.nz)*: the vines grow on the hillsides around the estate. On the *Wine Tours by Bike (from Renwick | tel. 03 572 7954 | winetoursbybike.co.nz)* you can travel from one estate to the next (hopefully, not in wiggly lines!), or discover new varieties by driving along the *Marlborough Wine Trail (wine-marlborough.co.nz)*. Lunch at the *Wairau River* winery *(daily 11.30am–3pm | 11 Rapaura Road | wairauriverwines.com | $$)* is a feast for the taste buds. Here, you can savour the region's many delicacies, including salmon and prawns. ⚐ *H10–11*

4 CAPE CAMPBELL
80km/90 mins from Picton (car)

The solitary, 100-year-old *lighthouse* on a rock spur in the sea played a starring role in the Hollywood film *The Light Between Oceans*, alongside Michael Fassbender and Alicia Vikander. The black-and-white circular building stands in total seclusion on the white cliffs of Clifford Bay. The only living creatures you'll meet here are fur seals on the beach.

At the foot of the lighthouse you can spend the night in the *cottage (NZ$180/night | 505 Cape Campbell Road | Seddon | tel. 021 183 9061 | experiencecape campbell.co.nz)* with a wooden veranda that was used in the film – it's incredibly romantic! ⚐ *H11*

INSIDER TIP
Sleep on a film set

CHRISTCHURCH

(⚐ F13) **In minutes, the beautiful and historic Christchurch was transformed to ruins. On 22 February 2011, 185 people were killed in a powerful earthquake, which caused the entire centre around the main Cathedral Square to more or less collapse.**

More than ten years later, South Island's biggest city (pop. 380,000) is slowly emerging from the rubble. But because Christchurch still looks a little like a giant construction site, a kind of earthquake tourism has developed in recent years. Kim McDonald offers a two-hour *Rebuild Walking Tour (from NZ$90 per person, NZ$30 for each additional person | kimsworld.co.nz)*, where you explore the historic ruins and learn about the reconstruction effort. The *Edmonds Band Rotunda*, a bandstand on the banks of the River Avon that was badly damaged in the earthquake, has been restored and was reopened in 2021. If you look

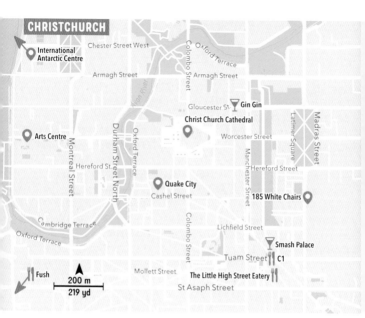

CHRISTCHURCH

International Antarctic Centre
Chester Street West
Colombo Street
Oxford Terrace
Armagh Street
Armagh Street
Avon River
Gloucester St
Gin Gin
Christ Church Cathedral
Worcester Street
Arts Centre
Durham Street North
Oxford Terrace
Montreal Street
Hereford St.
Manchester Street
Hereford Street
Latimer Square
Madras Street
Quake City
Cashel Street
185 White Chairs
Colombo Street
Lichfield Street
Cambridge Terrace
Oxford Terrace
Smash Palace
Tuam Street
C1
Fush
200 m
219 yd
Mollett Street
The Little High Street Eatery
St Asaph Street

beyond the depressed city centre, in Christchurch's suburbs you'll find fascinating and contrasting landscapes: long, wild sandy beaches on the east coast and the bustling *Lyttelton Harbour* at the heart of a green volcanic crater. The green heart of Christchurch beats just steps away from the city centre. The 🐦 *Botanic Gardens*, which are more than 150 years old, are home to plenty of native flora, while mighty oaks and sequoia trees tower majestically towards the sky and couples pose on the bridges over the Avon.

WHERE TO TO START?

Arts Centre: The historic building, which has been almost fully refurbished, is in a central location on Worcester Boulevard. From here, you can easily walk to most attractions in the city centre. A small, old-fashioned *Hop-on-Hop-off Tram* makes a circuit around the city centre. Most buses start from the Bus Interchange *(Lichfield/corner of Colombo Street)* and head in all directions, incl. the airport.

SIGHTSEEING

ARTS CENTRE 🏛️

Two-thirds of the Arts Centre, which was damaged by the earthquake, are now back in operation. The neo-Gothic building houses galleries showcasing contemporary New Zealand art, craft workshops and even a small cinema *(lumierecinemas.co.nz)*. Markets and markets concerts are held outside. *Daily 10am–5pm | 2 Worcester Blvd | artscentre.org.nz*

CHRISTCHURCH CATHEDRAL

Even in its ruined state, the Cathedral, dating from 1864, is still a city landmark and tourist magnet; before the quake it was the city's most visited attraction. The neo-Gothic church on *Cathedral Square* is an impressive monument to the devastating force of the 2011 earthquake. Rebuilding will cost over NZ$104 million and should be completed by 2028. Only five minutes away on foot, as a contrast, is the cardboard reconstruction of the ⚑ *Transitional Cathedral (daily 9am–5pm | 234 Hereford Street | cardboard cathedral.org.nz).*

QUAKE CITY

Interesting, multimedia exhibition at the *Canterbury Museum* about the earthquake and its repercussions. *Daily 10am–4pm | admission NZ$20 | 299 Durham Street North/corner of Armagh Street | canterburymuseum. com | ⏱ 1 hr*

185 WHITE CHAIRS

The empty white chairs created by artist Peter Majendie are a solemn memorial to the 185 earthquake victims. *Manchester/corner of Kilmore Street*

INTERNATIONAL ANTARCTIC CENTRE 🐧 ⛄

This is where things get uncomfortable … In a simulated Antarctic storm at minus 18°C, you experience close up what the New Zealand researchers

in the Antarctic have to endure, as well as plenty more about the South Pole. It's cute to watch feeding time for the funny little blue penguins. *Daily 9am–4pm | from NZ$49 | 38 Orchard Road | iceberg.co.nz | ⏱ 1.5 hrs*

EATING & DRINKING

C1

Cult café, where mouthwatering burger creations – *sliders* – are literally shot through high pressure hoses from the kitchen into the bar. Vegetarians and allergy-sufferers are also catered for. C1 supports sustainable projects in Samoa and roasts its own coffee. *Daily 7am–10pm | 185 High Street | c1espresso.co.nz | $*

FUSH

Every guest to come through the door is greeted with a friendly *"Kia Ora"* at this seafood joint. As well as serving up Kiwi classics such as green-lipped mussels and fish burgers, the family-run business focuses on *manaakitanga*, Maori hospitality. The seafood is all caught sustainably, and the fish & chips are quite rightly known as the best in town. **INSIDER TIP Deluxe fish & chips!** *Daily, noon–8.30pm | 104 the Runway | tel. 03 260 1177 | fushshore bro.co.nz | $*

THE LITTLE HIGH STREET EATERY

Eight eateries under one roof serving up pizza, sushi and Caribbean delicacies. *Daily 11am–10pm | 255 Asaph Street | tel. 0210 208 4444 | littlehigh. co.nz | $–$$*

SPORT & ACTIVITIES

MARGARET MAHY PLAYGROUND

The biggest playground in the southern hemisphere has something for everyone. Young or old, you can enjoy a bounce on the trampoline, cool off in the water fountains or use one of the electric barbecues in the picnic area. *177 Armagh Street*

WELLNESS

HE PUNA TAIMOANA

Five hot pools, each a different temperature, and a sauna with ocean view: The New Brighton Beach spa is the perfect spot to relax on a rainy day – or to warm up after a dip in the chilly Pacific. Plus, nearby is a popular water playground for the kids. *Daily 10am–7.30pm | 195 Marine Parade | adults NZ$19, children NZ$14 | tel. 03 941 7818 | hepunataimoana.co.nz*

FESTIVALS

BREAD & CIRCUS FESTIVAL

For ten days every April, *Victoria Square* is transformed into a stage for street performers from around the country. All free to watch with food trucks and a retro Ferris wheel to complete the appeal. *breadandcircus.co.nz*

NIGHTLIFE

GIN GIN

There's not much you won't want to photograph at this stylish cocktail bar, whether that's the candy-coloured

A picturesque lighthouse welcomes visitors into the harbour at Akaroa

interior that looks like something out of a Wes Anderson movie or the artfully decorated drinks. *Tue–Fri 4pm–1am, Sat–Sun 1pm–1am | 4–6 New Regent Street | gingin.co.nz*

SMASH PALACE

The Good Bye Blue Monday bar was destroyed in the 2011 earthquake before reopening two years later as Smash Palace. Made of old buses and containers, it is a prime destination for beer and burgers in Christchurch. Be sure to try the home-brewed *Boodgie Beer! Tue–Thu from 3pm, Fri/Sat noon until late, Sun noon–6pm | 172 High Street | thesmashpalace.co.nz*

AROUND CHRISTCHURCH

5 TRANZALPINE EXPRESS

4km/7 mins from the city centre to the train station in Addington (car)
Feet up, keep your eyes open: the train takes about five hours from Christchurch to Greymouth on the west coast – you travel across the sparse Canterbury Plains with deep blue, fast-flowing rivers, over high viaducts and past the impressive *Arthur's Pass* and snow-covered mountain summits. *Daily 8.15am from Christchurch Railway Station | 1 hr stop in Greymouth, departs 2.05pm, back in Christchurch 6pm | one way trip from NZ$139 | tel. 0800 872 467 | greatjourneysofnz.co.nz | ▥ E–F 12–13*

6 LYTTELTON HARBOUR

12km/15 mins from Christchurch (car)
You can spend a delightful half day in Lyttleton Harbour. Set in a volcanic crater, the harbour is surrounded by the 446-m-high *Port Hills*. From the summit you have a view filled with contrasts: in the west, the snow-covered South Alps and in the east, Banks Peninsula. The station for the *Christchurch Gondola (daily 10am–5pm | from NZ$35 | 10 Bridle Path Road | Heathcote Valley | christchurchattractions.nz)* is at SH 74 by the road tunnel to Lyttelton.

You can also cycle to the harbour from Christchurch, as there are plenty of mountain-bike routes in Port Hills *(onyourbike.co.nz)*: arrival through Lyttelton Tunnel *(Tunnel Road)* and return past the pleasant bathing locations of *Sumner* and *New Brighton* via the picturesque *Summit* and *Evans Pass Road*. A great restaurant on Sumner beach is *Beach Sumner (daily | 25 Esplanade | tel. 03 326 7226 | beachsumner.co.nz | $–$$). ▥ F13*

7 BANKS PENINSULA

70km/1 hr 10 mins from Christchurch (car)
The drive to the green, volcanic peninsula is already a feast for the eyes. In 1840, the French attempted to fight with the British over New Zealand on the peninsula. However, it was five days too late, as the Waitangi Treaty had already been signed. But the motto is still "Vive la France!" in the attractive harbour town of *Akaroa (akaroa.com)*. This Francophile atmosphere is effectively exploited for

Marine mammals come to feed in the rich waters around Kaikoura

tourists with the appropriate street names, baguettes and the annual *Frenchfest* in October. The *Boutique Bed & Breakfast French Bayhouse (frenchbayhouse.co.nz)*, housed in a wooden villa from 1874, offers plenty of French chic. The mosaic garden in the quaint *Giant's House (Oct–April daily 11am–4pm, May–Sept until 2pm | NZ$20.50 | 68 Rue Balguerie | thegiantshouse.co.nz | $$$)* is bright and cheerful and was created by the extravagant artist Josie Martin. Tip: it's best to avoid the garden on days when cruise ships have arrived in town. A good alternative is a hike to *Stony Bay Peak* over the crater rims of old volcanoes, where sheep now graze on the green hillsides. Pleasant

swimming beaches are in *Okains Bay* with a campsite and shop. The protected *natural harbour* of Akaroa is teeming with rare sea creatures – like the tiny Hector's dolphins; you can even swim alongside them or watch them on the *Black Cat Cruises (Akaroa Main Wharf | several tours daily: swimming NZ$199, animal watch NZ$95 | tel. 0800 937 946 | blackcat.co.nz).* *G13*

⑧ KAIKOURA ★

180km/2 hrs 25 mins from Christchurch (car)

The giant fin of a humpback whale glides majestically into the depths. Orcas, black dolphins and seabirds complete the ocean spectacle against a backdrop of snow-covered mountains in the Kaikoura Range. It's breathtaking! New Zealand's whale-watching mecca is a magnet for sea creatures because deep in Kaikoura Canyon, warm, subtropical water meets the cold Antarctic Sea, which produces a nutrient-rich "superfood" mix. Even the massive sperm whale has plenty to eat here. It can turn stormy, so it's best to go out on the water during the morning with 🏊 *Whale Watch Kaikoura (from NZ$150, children NZ$60 | Whaleway Station Road | tel. 0800 655 121 | whalewatch. co.nz)*. Alternatively, the sight of a whale from a helicopter is an unforgettable experience: whale-watching from the sky is available with *Kaikoura Helicopters (tel. 0800 455 4354 | worldofwhales.co.nz)*. At *Dolphin Encounter (96 Esplanade | tel. 0800 733 365 | dolphinencounter.co.nz)* there are several daily tours: swimming with dolphins from NZ$220.

If you prefer to get more active, then book a sunset kayak tour or get close to the inhabitants of the local seal colony by joining a pedal-kayak tour with *Seal Kayak Kaikoura (daily | from NZ$105, also guided family tours from NZ$105, children NZ$69 | 2 Beach Road | tel. 0800 387 7325 | sealkayakkaikoura.com)*.

The strong earthquake in 2016 cut off the small town of Kaikoura (pop. 2,000) for a long while. The ocean floor was raised by several metres, which had an effect on the ecosystem. But the whales and tourists have now returned. Kaikoura is a Maori word meaning "langoustine meal" – you can enjoy large portions five minutes from the city centre at the *Pier Hotel (1 Avoca Street | tel. 03 319 5037 | thepierhotel.co.nz | $–$$)* with mountain views. Lobster, mussels and crayfish for a more reasonable price are on offer at the popular food truck 🐷 *Nins Bin (daily 9am–9.30pm | State Highway 1 | FB: nins bin kai koura)*. Established in 1977, it's a real institution. *G12*

DUNEDIN

(D16) **Student culture meets colonial architecture: the university city is a mix of magnificent Victorian buildings dating from the period of the gold rush and student houses in need of refurbishment. The weather in Dunedin (pronounced Duneedin) is unpredictable: on some days, it's high summer in the morning and**

WHERE TO START?

Octagon: When the locals say: "I'm gonna go into town", they mean George Street with its shops and cafés, which leads to the main Octagon Square, where the roads peel off in all directions. The station, Toitu Otago Settlers Museum and St Paul's Cathedral are a short walk from here. Bus No. 8 travels to St Clair Beach and takes about 30 minutes (the bus stops on George Street).

DUNEDIN

Baldwin Street

Malvern

Evans St.

Botanic Garden

No 7 Balmac

Drivers Rd.
Elder St.
Bank Street

Otago Museum

Albany St.
Anzac Ave.
Butts Rd.

Arthur St.
Void
Experience Dunedin
Emerson's

Gallery de Novo
Railway Station
Toitu Otago Settlers Museum
Dog With Two Tails
Vogel St Kitchen
New New New Corporation
Starfish Café

Ilto
ma

Otago Harbour

Portobello Rd.

800 m
875 yd

how far south you are. You sense that Dunedin is at the bottom of the world where historic buildings are starting to decay because they're no longer required.

Then, the city comes alive again: for instance, on Saturdays when the eco-conscious sell their home-grown produce at the *Farmer's Market* at the station and bands play between the market stalls. With 20,000 students, the 130,000-strong city enjoys a vibrant café culture and live-music scene *(dunedinmusic.com)*. The quality of life is high: houses are (still) affordable; the people are super friendly, and you never have to drive for longer than 20 minutes to find the next empty beach.

autumn in the afternoon. But don't let that put you off visiting.

When the sun comes out in the former Scottish enclave (Dunedin is the old Gaelic name for Edinburgh), it makes the green undulating landscape glisten around New Zealand's old capital city. In summer, the surfers are still riding the waves at St Clair Beach at ten o'clock in the evening and then wax lyrical in the cafés along the promenade about the constant good *swell* in the world's most famous bay for surfers. The water rarely gets

INSIDER TIP
Warm pool in the cold ocean

warmer than 17°C, but it's pleasantly warm in the *Salt Water Pool* in the sea along the cliffs. Occasionally, seals and penguins rest on the rocks around the pool. It's a reminder of

SIGHTSEEING

EXPERIENCE DUNEDIN

On a trike for five people, Andrew Sim shows his guests the Otago Peninsula and the best corners of his hometown. With stops at the university, Chinese Gardens and railway station. *60 mins/NZ$75 | tel. 021 263 3261 | experiencedunedin.com*

RAILWAY STATION

Polite society in long dresses and top hats once paraded around the railway station built in Flemish neo-Renaissance style (1907). Today, tourists in colourful outdoor jackets wait for the *Dunedin Railways* (see p. 103) to carry them away them on various trips. *Anzac Av.*

TOITU OTAGO SETTLERS MUSEUM

What was it like inside the first migrant ships from Europe? How did the Maoris live after their arrival from Polynesia? The 100-year-old museum focuses on visualizing the early beginnings of people settling in Otago. *Daily 10am–5pm | free admission | 31 Queens Garden | toituosm.com | ⏱ 1.5 hrs*

OTAGO MUSEUM

Moa skeletons, Maori canoes and Sir Edmund Hillary's passport: the museum on several floors with its own planetarium offers a good insight into New Zealand's history. *Daily 10am–5pm | free admission or a donation | 419 Great King Street | otagomuseum.nz | ⏱ 2 hrs*

BOTANIC GARDEN

Tuis and bellbirds chatter in New Zealand's oldest botanical garden among gigantic redwoods and rhododendrons. There are fabulous views of the surroundings. On the meadow in front of the 100-year-old glasshouse, students leaf through their books. At the café *Croque-o-dile (daily 9.30am–4.30pm)* there are croques and crêpes on the menu. *Daily sunrise to sunset | 12 Opoho Road | dunedinbotanicgarden.co.nz*

BALDWIN STREET

Hardened rugby trainers, according to the *Guinness Book of Records*, let their players run up the steepest street in the world – and even tourists do their best not to get out of breath with a gradient of 35%. You need about ten minutes to go 350m. Fortunately, there's a fountain to drink from at the top.

EATING & DRINKING

You should definitely try the local craft beer, freshly caught *blue cod* and gourmet pies from *Who ate all the pies* at the *Farmer's Market (Sat 8am–12.30pm | at the station | otago farmersmarket. org.nz)*. The best cafés and restaurants are at the *Octagon*, in *George Street* and the *Esplanade* at *St Clair Beach*.

NO 7 BALMAC

Complete with its own vegetable and herb garden in trendy *Maori Hill*, this restaurant specializes in contemporary

Dunedin's 100-year-old railway station looks like a gingerbread house

New Zealand cuisine. The saltimbocca with Otago venison and the mushroom quinoa burger are sure hits! *Mon–Fri 7am–midnight, Sat 8am–midnight, Sun 8am–3pm | 7 Balmacewen Road | tel. 03 464 0064 | no7balmac.co.nz | $$*

STARFISH CAFÉ

You visit the café at St Clair Beach for the delicious fish tacos and numerous surfers. Every Friday, different bands play their guitars and drown out the noise of the surf. *Sun–Wed 6.30am–4pm, Thu–Sat 7am–11pm | tel. 03 455 5940 | starfishcafe.co.nz | $–$$*

VOGEL ST KITCHEN

Where a big graffiti fish decorates the house wall you enter the brick loft with vintage furniture and a display counter filled with delicious food like carrot cake, cheese rolls and beetroot salad. *Mon–Fri 7.30am–3pm, Sat/Sun 8.30am–4pm | 76 Vogel Street | tel. 03 477 3623 | vogelstkitchen.nz | $*

SHOPPING

GALLERY DE NOVO

Who says that art has to be expensive? Liz Fraser sells photographs, prints, sculptures and paintings in different price categories by young artists from New Zealand. Affordable souvenirs are the cool New Zealand travel posters by Lisa Nicole Moes. *Mon–Fri 9.30am–5.30pm, Sat/Sun 10am–3pm | 101 Stuart Street | gallerydenovo.co.nz*

VOID

So, you only packed practical outer-wear and want to emanate the cool look of surfers on the beach? In this streetwear shop young, relaxed

Surfers prize the reliable waves that roll into St Clair Beach

assistants help you choose board shorts, trainers and sunglasses. *Mon-Fri 9am-5.30pm, Sat 10am-5pm, Sun 11am-4pm | 8 Albion Lane | void.co.nz*

SPORT & ACTIVITIES

DUNEDIN RAILWAYS ☂

Aboard Dunedin Railways' trains, you'll travel through empty countryside – and feel as if you're travelling back in time, especially in the 1920s *Heritage Carriages*. Looking through the old wooden windows, you hardly notice any signs of modern life. Instead, there are deep gorges, wild rivers and rugged cliffs. While the train rattles along steep cliffs, you have a bird's-eye view of the ocean. There are several routes to choose from: the journey from Dunedin to Moeraki (p. 105) and back takes around five hours *(incl. a 2-hr stopover | NZ$68)*; the *Inlander Tour (3.5 hrs | NZ$60)* leads through isolated mountain landscapes to Hindon and back along the Taieri River Gorge; while *The Victorian (NZ$79)* day tour rattles along the ocean and back to Oamaru (p. 105), where you can visit the *Steam Punk HQ Museum*, for example. *Tel. 02 2436 9074 | dunedinrailways.co.nz*

SURFING

☂ *St Clair Beach* has the most reliable surf waves in New Zealand. In the wide bay there is a *Surf School (90 mins incl. board and neoprene suit NZ$70 | The Esplanade | tel. 0800 484 141 | espsurfschool.co.nz)* where you can hire the board and there is enough space for beginners to practise.

BEACHES

If you struggle to imagine a beach without a board and waves, you have to visit *St Clair Beach (see above)*. *Allans Beach* is also impressive with its craggy cliffs and seals surfing the waves. At *Smails Beach* you either brave the surf or look up from the dunes to the sheep on the high cliffs. To reach *Tunnel Beach*, walk down a steep slope and you'll be rewarded with a beach in the middle of high sandstone cliffs.

NIGHTLIFE

DOG WITH TWO TAILS 🐷

Bands test new songs; artists exhibit their works and anyone who wants can spontaneously sit at the piano. The café bar with a small stage, old leather sofas and bookshelves is an experimental showcase for anyone. *Tue-Thu 10am-9.30pm, Fri/Sat until midnight | Moray Place | dogwith twotails.co.nz*

> **INSIDER TIP**
> Open mic for young creatives

RIALTO CINEMA ☂

An insider tip for rainy days: in the cinema with an art deco foyer, it still looks like the 1930s. *11 Moray Place | tel. 03 474 2200 | rialto.co.nz*

BREWERIES

Chilli Pils and *Poppy Seed Ale*: the popular micro-brewery *New New New (218 Crawford Street | tel. 03 395 6445 | newnewnew.nz)* opens its tap room and its Asian *Yum Cat Diner* most days *(Wed–Fri 4–9pm, Sat noon–10pm and Sun noon–4pm)*. At *Emerson's (daily 10am–10pm | 70 Anzac Av. | tel. 03 477 1812 | emersons.co.nz | $$)* there is Indian Pale Ale and stout made in Dunedin. These go down well in the restaurant with steak, Merino lamb or freshly caught fish.

AROUND DUNEDIN

⁹ OTAGO PENINSULA

17km/25 mins from Dunedin (car)

Heading along Highcliff Road in Dunedin to the peninsula, you will constantly want to stop and take photos. From the crest of the hill you overlook Otago Harbour, green Hobbit hills and cruise ships on the horizon. If you turn right into Seal Point Road, there's another reason to grab your camera: *yellow-eyed penguins* on the beach at Sandfly Bay; they usually appear late in the afternoon.

It's worth ordering a portion of fish & chips in the historic *1908 Café (Wed–Sun noon–2pm and 5.30–8pm, Mon noon–2pm | 7 Harington Point Road | tel. 03 478 0801 | 1908cafe.co.nz | $)* in the small coastal town of Portobello, before heading for the world's only *mainland colony of albatrosses (daily from 11.30am to twilight, in winter from 10.30am | NZ$52 | tel. 03 478 0499 | albatross.org.nz)*. On a guided tour *(1 hr)* you can watch the rare birds with a wingspan of up to 3.5m

through binoculars. To get closer to the birds, take a boat tour on the *MV Monarch (1 hr | NZ$57 | wildlife.co.nz)*, which departs from Wellers Rock Wharf.

If you want to explore wildlife on the peninsula with a local expert, you should book a *Cross Country Ride* with "Peninsula Dundee" aka Perry Reid of *Natures Wonders Otago (1 hr | NZ$99 | tel. 03 478 1150 | natureswonders.co.nz)*. The committed nature conservationist takes you to the beaches with penguins and seals in small all-wheel drive vehicles. In the evening, you travel on the winding Portobello Road along the waterfront in Otago Harbour back to Dunedin.

In 1967, when Barry and Margaret Barker from Wellington purchased 🌂 *Larnach Castle (daily 9am–7pm | NZ$37 | 145 Camp Road | larnachcastle.co.nz)* on Otago Peninsula 15km east of Dunedin, the castle with its panoramic view of Otago Harbour was a ruin. Today, the former private villa, "New Zealand's unique castle", is a museum. The interior is a reminder of the time when Australian banker William Larnach had the building constructed between 1873 and 1886. Four-poster beds made from exotic woods are in the bedrooms and chandeliers hang from the ceilings. Every day at 2pm, 2.30pm and 3pm (just like the old days) high tea is served in the well-manicured garden (book in advance). In *Larnach Castle Lodge (12 rooms | tel. 03 476 1616 | larnachcastle.co.nz | $$$)* next to the castle you can spend the night in various themed rooms in four-poster beds

Moeraki Boulders: four-million-year-old stepping stones on Koekohe Beach

and old wooden carriages – many rooms have a bird's-eye view of Otago Harbour. *E16*

🔟 MOERAKI BOULDERS
75km/1 hr from Dunedin (car)

Are they alien brains? Or bowls belonging to giants? There are many legends surrounding over 50 round boulders at Koekohe Beach north of Dunedin. In fact, the stones are about four million years old and were formed by a unique natural phenomenon. According to geologists, the up-to-2m-wide mega-marbles grow out of the stone on the beach, which is rich in minerals, and was once on the seabed. You can take some quick photos of the boulders. Afterwards, you should definitely dine at *Fleur's*

Place *(Wed–Sun from 9.30am | tel. 03 439 4480 | fleursplace.com | $$)* in the picture-postcard harbour of *Moeraki*. Fishing boats bring their catch directly to the local quay, and chef Fleur Sullivan creates delicious dishes, which have earned her a countrywide reputation, with langoustines, cod and gurnets. *E15*

🔟 OAMARU
115km/1 hr 25 mins from Dunedin (car)

Stranger than fiction: the quiet little town, which is well known for *little blue penguins* and Victorian architecture, has recently become the world's capital for the steampunk movement. Fans of this sub-culture wear Victorian costumes and use antiques to make futuristic sculptures or steam-driven vehicles. The annual *Steampunk Festival* (see p. 25) in May already made it into the *Guinness Book of Records* thanks to scores of international visitors. The historic centre, the *Harbour & Tyne Historic Precinct (victorianoamaru.co.nz)*, with its white limestone Victorian buildings, is a backdrop for the movement. There is now a *Steam Punk HQ Museum (daily 10am–4pm | NZ$10, children NZ$2 | 1 Humber Street | steampunkoamaru. co.nz | ⊙ 1 hr)* located here and a 🛝 playground in the nostalgic style of the subculture.

One of New Zealand's best craft beers is brewed just around the corner at *Scotts Brewing Co. (daily from 11am | 1 Wansbeck Street | scottsbrewing. co.nz | $)* – it has a lovely beer garden and serves crispy stonebaked pizza! At sunset, from here it's just a few minutes' walk to the *Little Blue Penguins Colony (evening viewing in summer from approx. 8.30pm | NZ$15 | 2 Waterfront Road | penguins.co.nz)*. ⊞ E15

🔢 CATLINS ★

115km/1 hr 3 0 mins from Dunedin to Catlins Lake (car)

Where the wild things are: at sunset, penguins hop out of the sea and seals chase you along the beach. The *Catlins* are south of Dunedin (see p. 148) between Kaka Point and Fortrose: an unspoilt, windswept region, where you meet more animals than people. At *Roaring Bay*, you can spot plenty of yellow-eyed *penguins (information: doc.govt.nz)*, and at *Nugget Point* there is a seal colony below the lighthouse. Hiking trails lead through the rainforest to waterfalls such as the *Purakaunui* or *Matai Falls*. On the beach at 🐷 *Porpoise Bay*, if you're lucky during the surfing course *(catlinssurf.co.nz)*, Hector's dolphins jump with you through the waves, and in *Curio Bay* at low tide a fossilized forest, the *Jurassic Petrified Forest*, is exposed. At Kaka Point, you can stay overnight in typical New Zealand *cribs* as the locals' holiday houses are called on South Island. From the Eco Retreat *Mohua Park* in Tawanui, the three- to four-hour tours begin with *Catlins Scenic & Wildlife (NZ$125, children NZ$60 | tel. 03 415 8613 | catlins mohuapark.co.nz)*; you track penguins and seals with local guides. ⊞ C–D 16–17

STEWART ISLAND

(⊞ B17–18) **If you want to make the trip to Rakiura, the "island of glowing skies", as ★ Stewart Island is known by the Maoris, you must be keen: the journey over the choppy, 32-km-wide Foveaux Strait, the unpredictable weather and total seclusion don't tempt everyone.**

The island is almost as big as Tenerife, but only about 400 people live there – all in the settlement of *Oban*. The rest of the island is unspoilt wilderness that still looks the same as it did thousands of years ago. The dense rainforest of 🚩 *Rakiura National*

Park is the habitat for some 20,000 kiwis, because here they hardly have any predators such as cats, rats and possums. The emerald-green sea sparkles invitingly in the summer sunshine, but it's ice cold.

There are only 20km of roads, but 200km of hiking trails through unspoilt nature, where you'll often see penguins waddling across the road. Things are done differently on Raikura. Children learn at school to spend the night on their own in the rainforest, and the island's only policeman must repeatedly warn his fellow citizens to not just borrow someone else's cars – on the island, it's common to leave the key in the ignition. If you're lucky, on Stewart Island you can see the ⚑ *Aurora Australis (forecasts: aurora-service.net)*, the southern lights – even in summer.

SIGHTSEEING

RAKIURA MUSEUM ⚑ 🐄

Sperm whale teeth and portraits of emaciated emigrants: here, you get an impression of how hard life must have been for the early settlers and whalers on Stewart Island. *Mon–Fri 10am– 4pm, Sat/Sun 10am–3pm | NZ$10 | 11 Main Road | Oban | stewart island.co.nz | ⏱ 1 hr*

ULVA ISLAND

On the uninhabited island, birds that are extinct elsewhere tune up for proper concerts. "Bird whisperer" Ulva, a descendant of the first Maoris on Stewart Island, helps with the search for rare *kaka parrots* and flightless *wekas*. Kiwis occasionally turn up here during the daytime too. Half-day tour incl. water taxi *(NZ$145 | tel. 03 219 1216 | ulva.co.nz)* from Golden Bay

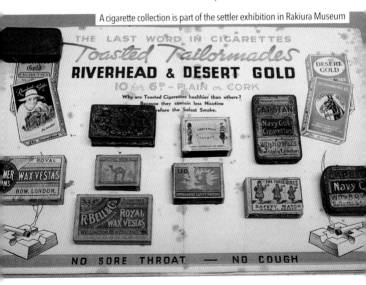

A cigarette collection is part of the settler exhibition in Rakiura Museum

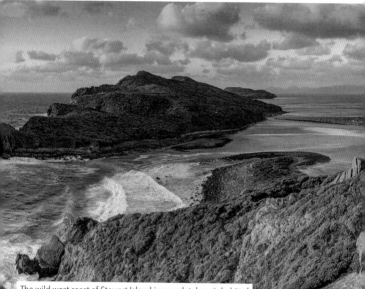

The wild west coast of Stewart Island is completely uninhabited

Wharf (15-minutes' walk from the ferry wharf in Oban).

SPORT & ACTIVITIES

BIRDWATCHING

If you're new to birdwatching, be inspired by *Angela Steffens'* enthusiasm for birds. On a five-hour water-taxi tour, she will invite you to follow little blue penguins on Maori beach and watch the sooty shearwaters that fly back to land in the evening. *Nov–March | NZ$260 | tel. 02 7316 3077 | beaksandfeathers.co.nz*

RAKIURA TRACK

As there are only 20km of roads on Stewart Island, you must explore the rest of the island on foot. For instance, on the 36-km-long *Rakiura Track*, which in three days takes you from Lee Bay to Fern Gully. You hike through dense rainforest across walkways and along secluded beaches. At night-time, you sleep in huts with wood ovens *(booking.doc.govt.nz)* and hear kiwis rustling in the bush. The tour starts in Lee Bay, 7km north of Oban.

WILD KIWI ENCOUNTER

When kiwis use their long beaks at night to hunt for fleas in the sand, you have a very good chance of spotting one. *Real Journeys* takes you by boat at sunset to one of the island's remote parts, where you join guides to go looking for these timid birds. Please note: seals sleep in the dunes and don't want to be disturbed! | *NZ$199 | realnz.com|* ⏱ *4 hrs*

are collected from here again in the evening. And, between you and me, this unique experience costs about the same as the kiwi-spotting tour. *Approx. NZ$175 | from Oban | tel. 03 218 9129 | stewartislandflights.com*

NIGHTLIFE

SOUTH SEA HOTEL

Photos of crashed aircraft and whales cut open adorn the walls, while men with bronzed faces stand at the bar: it's party time at the bottom of the world! In the island's only pub, tourists and island residents dance spontaneously among the tables or sit at the piano. The highlight every Sunday is the pub quiz, where in 2015 Prince Harry even participated during his tour of the Commonwealth. Deep-fried green-lipped mussels taste good with the beer. *26 Elgin Terrace | Oban | tel. 03 219 1059 | stewart-island.co.nz | $$*

GETTING THERE

From Bluff, you can travel for one hour in the catamaran *Foveaux Express (up to 4 times daily depending on season | NZ$85 one way | tel. 03 212 7660 | realnz.com)* over the waves and oyster beds to Stewart Island. The strait is famous for its stormy weather so it's a good idea to bring seasickness tablets! From Invercargill, you can fly to *Stewart Island (3 times daily | NZ$225 return trip | tel. 03 218 9129 | stewartislandflights.com).*

BEACHES

BATHING BEACH ☀️🌴

This sheltered bay complete with golden sand is just a 15-minute walk along the path from Oban. The rainforest brushes against the edge of the beach and the air is filled with the sound of tuis and bellbirds. The water might be crystal clear, but it's also freezing cold. Best to warm up in the sun before attempting to swim!

MASON BAY

Kiwis and pure solitude

In the wide bay, you won't meet any people, but instead you'll encounter more kiwis than anywhere else in New Zealand. You land on the wide sandy beach in a light propeller aircraft and

AROUND STEWART ISLAND

🔢 BLUFF

40km/1 hr from Oban (ferry)

A small coastal town with weather-beaten wooden houses. The only luxury in the area are the bountiful oysters in the sea *(March-Aug)*. With a photo from *Stirling Point* you can prove to your friends that you made it to the bottom of the world. A sign says that from here it's only another 4,810km to the South Pole. 📖 *C17*

🔢 INVERCARGILL

40km/1 hr from Oban (ferry), then 25km/25 mins (car)

Just before you fall into the sea at New Zealand's southernmost point, there is another town that only a handful of visitors pay attention to. Invercargill, with its chequerboard layout and population of 55,000, at first looks rather dreary. But if you look more closely, you discover magnificent Victorian buildings in the whole of the town, for example, the 1889 *Water Tower* or the *Civic Theatre* from 1906. The residents are proud of their museum *Transport World (daily 10am–5pm | NZ$35 | 491 Tay Street | transportworld.co.nz | ⏱ 2 hrs)*, which has one of the world's biggest

In fine weather you won't need a filter for your photographs of stunning Milford Sound

collections of classic cars. The *Fat Bastard Pies (Mon–Fri 6.30am–4pm | 158 Tay Street | $)* are considered the best in the country. *▢ C17*

15 RIVERTON
40km/1 hr from Oban (ferry), then 65km/55 mins (car)

A small artists' eco-community with fishing harbour and light wooden houses. Locals rent out holiday houses *(bookabach.co.nz)* on the long sandy beach. In the *Te Hikoi Museum (Oct–March daily 10am–5pm, April–Sept 10am–4pm | NZ$8 | 172 Palmerston Street | tehikoi.co.nz | ⏱ 1.5 hrs)* everything is about the close relationship between Maoris and European settlers at New Zealand's southern tip. Reconstructions of old huts and whaling boats make the past come alive. On *Gemstone Beach*, 30km further north, you can find semiprecious stones like quartz and jade on the beach. *▢ B17*

TE ANAU

(▢ B15) **Tranquil Te Anau on Lake Te Anau is the starting point for tours through Fiordland, New Zealand's biggest national park.**

Behind South Island's biggest lake you can already see the summits of the UNESCO World Natural Heritage Site soaring upwards. In the cafés you can listen to the hikers' expedition tales. Large swathes of the national park, which is about half the size of Sicily, are still unexplored and belong only to the Fiordland penguins, dolphins, kea parrots and sandflies. Humans are only guests in this wilderness world – on Milford and Doubtful sounds, or on the three Great Walks: the Milford, Routeburn and Kepler tracks.

SIGHTSEEING

GLOW-WORM CAVES 👥
By boat, it takes 30 minutes from Te Anau to reach a glow-worm cave. This is a fascinating underworld where the green glow of the mosquito larvae provide light and the waterfalls cascade in the darkness. In small boats, you explore the meandering river system inside the caves with *Real NZ (duration 2.5 hr incl. transport | NZ$99, children NZ$35 | tel. 0800 656 501 | realnz.com)*.

SPORT & ACTIVITIES

HIKING TOURS
Do you want to explore nature alone, or with a guide? For just a few hours, or several days? Three Great Walks are possible from Te Anau. The best known is the *Milford Track*, which the first settlers built in 1880 to travel from Lake Te Anau to Milford Sound. The popular tour takes four days with stopovers in huts. You should definitely book several months in advance at *Fiordland National Park Visitor Centre (hut NZ$110/night | no camping | tel. 03 249 7924 | greatwalks.co.nz)*. The same applies for the *Kepler Track (hut NZ$102, tent pitch NZ$32/night)*, a 60km circuit, which takes three to four

days through valleys formed by glaciers and mountains with views of Lake Te Anau. The track begins and ends at Kepler car park, 5km from Te Anau, and is suitable for day trips (e.g. along Waiau River as far as Rainbow Reach). The *Routeburn Track (huts NZ$130, tent pitch NZ$40/night)* heads in the direction of Mount Aspiring National Park through an alpine wonderland with waterfalls and majestic summits. You need two to four days for the 33km from The Divide Shelter on Milford Road (85km from Te Anau) to the Routeburn Shelter near Glenorchy. *Trips & Tramps (tel. 03 249 7081 | tripsandtramps. com)* organize guided day trips along the Great Walks.

AROUND TE ANAU

🔟 DOUBTFUL SOUND

2 hrs from Te Anau (boat and bus)

Three times longer and more difficult to reach, Doubtful Sound has more channels and is less touristy than Milford Sound. As no road goes to the 40km-long fjord, you have to depend on tour operators. They will take you by boat across Lake Manapouri and then by bus over Wilmot Pass to the ferry wharf at Doubtful Sound. On the fjord you are unlikely to meet another boat, and the famous *Sound of Silence* in this area is better to listen to than on Milford Sound. The countryside is so beautiful that it is tempting to look

at it through the camera viewfinder. But then you're guaranteed to miss the moment when the dolphin jumps out of the water. You can occasionally pack away your equipment and enjoy what photos cannot capture: the fragrance of the dense green, the humid air and the graceful mountain giants.

A day trip incl. cruise in the sound costs about *NZ$199* or a two-day tour incl. kayak tour, buffet dinner and an overnight stay in a double cabin on the ship is about NZ$599 – both with *Real NZ (tel. 032 496 000 | realnz. com)*. Tip: before you depart, stay overnight in the historic *Murrell's Grand View House (4 rooms | Murrell Avenue | Manapouri | tel. 03 249 6642 | murrells.co.nz | $$$)*, which is 20 minutes by car from Te Anau. This is a B & B in a historic wooden villa with a priceless view of Lake Manapouri. 🏷 A15

🔢 MILFORD SOUND ★

120km/1 hr 30 mins from Te Anau (car)

Milford Sound in fine or bad weather is like the difference between colour and black-and-white photography: in the sunshine, the moss-covered cliff faces of the 15-km-long fjord shine a luminous green colour, the rainbows glisten in the numerous waterfalls, and when dolphins jump out of the bright blue water, nature looks as chocolate-box beautiful as a spray-paint mural. If it rains, suddenly the landscape only consists of grey tones. The mountain peaks disappear into the clouds and the water looks black; this too has its own special drama. With 200 rainy days and up to 8m of

Sea birds still outnumber the human visitors to Doubtful Sound

rain per annum the chances are high that you will arrive on a grey day. But you shouldn't miss the chance to take a boat trip into the mountains. The 1,692-m-high *Mitre Peak* on the fjord soars like a cathedral into the sky and the passengers on the excursion boats gasp "Amazing" and "Breathtaking". Arriving via Milford Road in a mountain setting filled with waterfalls, lakes and rivers is also an awesome spectacle. However, be prepared to share *Milford Sound* with plenty of other people.

You can choose from a variety of trips: for example, a two-hour tour to *Tasman Sea (NZ$89 | tel. 03 249 8110 | mitrepeak.com)*; an overnight cruise incl. travel, kayak tour, buffet dinner

and accommodation in a double cabin on the *Fiordland Navigator (NZ$399 | tel. 03 249 6000 | realnz.com)*; or a kayak tour at sunrise to the highest waterfall, *Lady Bowens Falls (2 hr | NZ$115 | tel. 0800 476 726 | roscosmilfordkayaks.com)*.

You can enjoy real silence on paddle tours incl. a short hike along the *Milford Track (1 hr kayak tour and 3.5-hr hike | NZ$135 | tel. 0800 476 726 | roscosmilfordkayaks.com)*. The only option to stop overnight in the area is *Milford Sound Lodge (milford lodge.com)* which has rooms and attractive chalets at a variety of prices. Don't forget to fill the car with petrol before departing in Te Anau! *B14*

QUEENSTOWN

(🔲 C15) **It's best to head to the ★ Queenstown waterfront first where everything is concentrated in a central location. You'll encounter adventure sports enthusiasts, buskers, backpackers and a spectacular natural setting.**

Lake Wakatipu sparkles light blue and the jagged cliffs of the Remarkables mountain range give the scenery its unique dramatic quality. You instantly feel compelled to see and do a whole host of things. Bungy jumping, parachuting or a ride in a speedboat? In the "world's adventure capital", it's difficult to decide what thrilling activities you should do first. You can escape the hustle and bustle on the *T.S.S. Earnslaw*, a 1912 steamer, which departs at a relaxed pace from the waterfront several times daily. Out on the lake you can admire the natural surroundings which are truly breathtaking.

SIGHTSEEING

BOB'S PEAK
From an altitude of 450m, you will feast your eyes on the panoramic vista over Lake Wakatipu. The climb will take you 60 minutes on the Tiki Trail, or you can take the *cable car (start Brecon Street)* up the mountain. At the summit, hiking trails and 12 different mountain-bike tracks invite you to explore the great outdoors. But it's also fine to sit in the *Skyline Café* and enjoy the views of Coronet Peak and

the Remarkables. You can make the descent either in a 🚠 bobsled, *The Luge (daily from 10am | includes 5 rides | NZ$67, children over five NZ$49 | tel. 03 441 0101 | skyline.co.nz)*, over a winding racing track, or else with a *tandem paragliding flight (NZ$219 | tel. 0800 759 688 | nzgforce.com)*. If you make the ascent after dark, you can enjoy some *stargazing (NZ$99 incl. gondola ride | from Skyline Gondola Station Brecon Street | skyline. co.nz)* and admire the countless stars of the southern hemisphere.

GIBBSTON VALLEY WINE
So, you think wine tasting is elitist and boring? This vineyard will surprise you as there are no wine snobs here; instead, there is a party atmosphere among the green hills. The restaurant hosts stag parties and several thousand visitors attend the annual summer concert with international stars in January. You must also try the cheese from the in-house dairy! *Daily 10am–5pm | 1820 State Highway 6 | tel. 03 442 6910 | gibbstonvalleynz.com*

EATING & DRINKING

THE BESPOKE KITCHEN
In the bright restaurant, which is popular with young travellers, the food tastes as good as it looks (muesli with floral deco!). It's also super healthy, as the ingredients for the halloumi burgers and smoothie bowls are from local organic farms. On the terrace, you feel far away from the busy crowds on the waterfront. *Daily*

Forget extreme sports – enjoy the landscape in a more relaxing way at the Skyline Café

8am–5pm | 9 Isle Street | tel. 03 409 0552 | bespokekitchen.co.nz | $

THE COW PIZZA

Many restaurants in Queenstown are located in modern buildings and consequently lack atmosphere. But not here! In the old cow shed, you sit at rustic wooden tables by candlelight and almost feel as you're in a Swiss ski chalet. The mix of pizza, pasta, beer and loud music has been a success for 40 years. Daily noon–11pm | Cow Lane | tel. 03 442 8588 | the cowpizza.co.nz | $

RATA

The decor includes plenty of wood and large paintings of the moss-covered rainforest: in the restaurant run by star chef Josh Emett you'll feel as if you're surrounded by nature. You'll choose between fine New Zealand dishes such as whitebait ceviche from the west coast, squid from Bluff or mussels from Cloudy Bay. Special tip: try the particularly tender Te Mana lamb from New Zealand's high mountains. Daily noon–10pm | 43 Ballarat Street | tel. 03 442 9393 | ratadining.co.nz | $$$

SHOPPING

VESTA

Queenstown's shopping streets are mostly uninspiring with lamb fleece stores and branches of international chains. Fortunately, there are exceptions like this original design shop in the oldest cottage in Queenstown that sells art prints, jewellery and lamps made by New Zealand artists. *Mon-Sat 10am–5pm | 19 Marine Parade | vestadesign.co.nz*

THE WALK IN WARDROBE

Tourists from around the world take their used clothing to the "preloved fashion boutique". The choice of international brands is particularly large. *Daily 10am–6pm | Beech Tree Arcade | 34 Shotover Street | thewalk inwardrobe.co.nz*

THE WINERY

Try the boutique wines from small wineries in New Zealand. You can also send your selection back home from here. *Mon–Thu 3–9pm, Fri/Sat noon–10pm, Sun 12am–8pm | 9 Ballarat Street | thewinery.co.nz*

SPORT & ACTIVITIES

In Queenstown, there are numerous possibilities for adventure – e.g. horizontal bungy jumping. The world's highest human catapult, the *Nevis Catapult (NZ$275 | Gibbston | tel. 0800 286 4958 | bungy.co.nz)* propels you up to 100kmh at a height of 150m across a gorge. Immediately next to this, you can jump from a height of 134m with your feet secured by a traditional *bungy line (NZ$275 | same provider)* from a cabin over the gorge towards the Nevis River. Free fall for 8.5 seconds! *Hydro Attack* is the name of a *speed boat (NZ$145 | Beach Street | tel. 27 477 9074 | hydroattack. co.nz)* in the shape of a shark which races at 80kmh across the lake, dives underwater and finally shoots straight up in the air out of the water like a jumping fish.

In the 👥 *Shotover Jet (NZ$129, children NZ$67 | tel. 0800 746 868 | shotoverjet.com)* you speed towards the cliff faces of steep canyons only to veer away and avert a collision at the very last minute. The ultimate adrenalin kick is made up of the "awesome foursome" *(information at combos. co.nz)*: Nevis bungy, a ride with the Shotover Jet, helicopter flight to Skippers Canyon and rafting on Shotover River for a total of NZ$720 – everything in one day.

Does the sound of that make you feel dizzy? Then take things at a more leisurely pace: a fabulous experience of the great outdoors is *packrafting (8–10 hrs | from NZ$350 | pack raftingnz.com)*: with a foldable canoe in a rucksack you trek across the empty *Reese Valley*, 45km north of Queenstown, and canoe on secluded rivers to an area that is called "paradise" for good reason. Or use the many *mountain-bike trails* around Queenstown. The brochure *Mountain Bike Riding* informs you about the best routes and is available from the Department of Conservation. Mountain bikes and e-bikes are available for hire from *Bikes & Beyond (Terrace Junction/Frankton Road | tel. 02 2125 2100 | bikesandbeyond. co.nz)*.

INSIDER TIP
Paddle into paradise

On the *Welcome Rock Trail*, 70km south of Queenstown, you cycle on private land away from the crowds and through the mountains. On the way,

Bungy jumping is just one of many ways to get your adrenalin pulsing in Queenstown

you can stay overnight in one of the old *gold-miner's huts (from NZ$138/ night | tel. 02 7239 2628 | welcome rock.co.nz)*. When it snows from June/ July, Queenstown's ski regions *Coronet Peak* and *The Remarkables* open for about three months.

T. S. S. EARNSLAW 🎭 ⚑

The 1912 vintage steamer is to Queenstown what the Eiffel Tower is to Paris. Six times daily the *Lady of the Lake*, with her smoking funnel, departs on a 90-minute tour of Lake Wakatipu. If you want, you can get off at the *Walter Peak Station* and watch one of the sheep-shearing shows – or enjoy horse-riding (40-minute tour with guide) in the great outdoors. The tour company is *Real Journeys (from*

NZ$70, children NZ$35 | Steamer Wharf / 88 Beach Street | tel. 0800 656 501 | realnz.com).

WELLNESS

ONSEN HOT POOLS 🌂

The view of the mountains is even more enjoyable if you're surrounded by warm bubbles. The wooden tubs filled with mountain water are on the cliffs above Shotover River and are separated from each other by wooden partition walls. You can book each pool for up to four people. *Daily 9am–11pm | Two-person pool NZ$150 | 160 Arthurs Point Road | tel. 03 442 5707 | onsen.co.nz*

Arrowtown dates back to the gold rush

AROUND QUEENSTOWN

18 ARROWTOWN

20km/20 mins from Queenstown (car)

If you can imagine the place without the souvenir shops, then Arrowtown, north of Queenstown, still resembles the gold-digger town that it once was. Old wooden houses and shops with saloon façades line Buckingham Street, and on Arrow River there are still the same huts in the forest that were once owned by Chinese gold prospectors. The river, which is crossed by the black riders in *Lord of the Rings*, is overgrown by trees has plenty of beautiful swimming spots. You can still pan for gold dust in the water here (the pans are available to hire on site). *C15*

19 WANAKA

70km/1 hr from Queenstown (car)

Nature takes over on Lake Wanaka and has a calming effect. It's just as picturesque as Queenstown, but no jet boats speed across the glacier lake, and paragliders only occasionally float from the mountains. On shady pebble beaches you can spend the day dosing and enjoying a refreshing swim in the clear water. *Bremner Bay*, *Dublin Bay* and *Glendhu Bay* (hire a stand-up paddle board) are especially beautiful. Or you can visit the island of *Mou Waho* and go swimming in a lake which glistens light green and deserves the name of Paradise Lake. Tours are offered by *Eco Wanaka*

NIGHTLIFE

ATLAS BEER CAFE

The bar is small, but the choice of craft beer is wide. Try unusual beers like *Yeastie Bo* or *Parrot Dog*, and enjoy a drink at the bar with the many locals and a lake view! *Mon–Fri 4pm–1am, Sat/Sun noon–1am | 88 Beach Street | atlasbeercafe.com*

THE LODGE BAR

A lake view, selected wines and interiors reminiscent of a luxury hunting lodge. In the bar of the New Zealand outdoor label Rodd & Gunn, meat pies and oysters are served with Pinot Noir and Sauvignon Blanc. Sometimes it's nice to be enjoy a touch of class! *Mon–Thu from 4pm, Fri–Sun from noon | 2 Rees Street | roddandgunn.com*

Adventure (4 hrs | NZ$255 | tel. 0800 926 326 | ecowanaka.co.nz). A popular hiking route takes about 45 minutes to Mount Iron, 250m above Wanaka. The ascent to Mount Roy (1,500m) is more exhausting. You complete the ascent and descent in about seven or eight hours, but your reward is a magnificent view of Mount Aspiring.

One museum that's fun for all the family is the 🛩 🎎 National Transport and Toy Museum (daily 8.30am–5pm | NZ$20, children NZ$5 | 891 Wanaka-Luggate Highway | nttmuseumwanaka. co.nz | ⏱ 1 hr). Adults can marvel at old aircraft and vintage cars (e.g. Chevrolets from the 1930s), while children can enjoy New Zealand's largest Barbie collection and over 1,000 Star Wars figurines. It goes without saying that there's also a toy shop at the end.

The food trucks in the centre of Wanaka (51 Brownston Street) on the south shore of the lake offer plenty of appetizing food, like Burrito Craft (daily noon–9pm | burritocraft.co.nz | $) or Francesca's Italian Kitchen (daily 4–9pm | fransitalian.co.nz | $). A few steps away is the Cinema Paradiso (72 Brownston Street | paradiso.net.nz), a cinema theatre filled with sofas. The tour operator Roam Wanaka (NZ$350 for a group of up to 6 people | roamwanaka.com) takes you to the best vineyards in the area.

The Blue Pools, 90 minutes by car north of Wanaka, are incredibly beautiful. From the road, it's a 30-minute walk to the bathing pools with

LORD OF THE RINGS HYPE

New Zealand is the cult destination for Hobbit fans. The Lord of the Rings and Hobbit trilogies were filmed in New Zealand.

There are countrywide LOTR tours (Lord of the Rings), on which you can cross off one dramatic and pictur-esque location after the next. However, it's cheaper to design your own tour. The Department of Conservation (DOC) has compiled a list of film locations in conservation areas: doc.govt.nz. Most of them are around Queenstown. For a start, drive up Mount Cardrona to get an impressive view of "Middle Earth". Straight ahead between the moun-tains is "Dimrill Dale". In Arrowtown, you follow the trail of Bilbo, Gandalf and the dwarves along the Arrow River and to the "Ford of Bruinen".

Dart River Safaris offer tours on the water and on horseback from Glenorchy; Heli Glenorchy (heli glenorchy.co.nz) offers aerial tours of the locations. You can get your magic ring in Nelson from Jens Hansen (see p. 130).

The Weta Workshop Studios (see p. 82) in Wellington offer a glimpse behind the scenes and into the world of film prop assistants and anima-tion artists. If you want to take photos with authentic LOTR scenery, then head for the "Shire" in Hobbiton (p. 67), near Matamata.

bright blue water in a rocky gorge in the rainforest. The skiing areas *Treble Cone* and *Cardrona* are open from June/July to early September, depending on the weather. *C14*

⓴ GLENORCHY

45km/45 mins from Queenstown (car)

The area around Glenorchy could be called "Middle Earth" because of the numerous *Lord of the Rings* film locations. The Road to Paradise from Queenstown leads to the small town at the north end of Lake Wakatipu. On the edge of Mount Aspiring National Park, where "Lothlorien", "Isengard" and "Amon Hen" film locations are situated, the landscape is indeed like

a paradise – and it's very secluded. You can spend several hours exploring the long tributary of the Dart River on funyaks (inflatable canoes) *(NZ$319, children NZ$229 incl. lunch and jeep tour to locations from* Lord of the Rings *and* X-Men *| dartriver.co.nz). B–C15*

㉑ MOUNT ASPIRING NATIONAL PARK

70km/1 hr 10 mins from Queenstown
Routeburn Shelter car park (car)

Mount Aspiring is New Zealand's Matterhorn. It towers 3,000m skywards and New Zealand's second largest national park is named after it. The park extends from Haast Pass to Lake Wakatipu and has impressive

Hikers' dreams come true in Mount Aspiring National Park

expansive valleys, glaciers, waterfalls and crystal-clear rivers. Famous hiking trails are the *Routeburn Track (in summer, book lodging in advance on doc.govt.nz | starting point car park at Routeburn Shelter)* and *Caples Track (buy the Backcountry Hut Pass in advance in a Doc Office | starting point car park at the end of Greenstone Road, 86km north of Queenstown)*. Tip: it's less busy on the tracks from Makaroa (130km north of Queenstown). For example, on *Gillespies Pass* or *Wilkin Valley* with ascent to *Top Forks Hut*.

On the half-day *Rob Roy Glacier Track (starting point at Raspberry Creek Carpark, 54km west of Wanaka, 120km north of Queenstown on the Wanaka–Mt Aspiring Road)*, you hike through the valley by the Matukituki River, past waterfalls and to the glacier below Mount Rob Roy. At the view-point, keas (parrots) wait for your lunch.

If you want to see as much as possible in a short time (and don't want to hike for very long), book the *Siberia Experience (NZ$455 | tel. 03 443 4385 | siberiaexperience.co.nz)*, a four-hour fly/hike/jet boat tour which begins in Makaroa. *B–C14*

AORAKI/ MOUNT COOK

(D13) **Unfortunately, the summit of Aoraki (Mount Cook), the "mountain that pierces the clouds", is usually hidden behind clouds.**

With a little luck, New Zealand's white giant (3,724m) will be gleaming in the sunshine – and while you hike around the country's highest mountain you'll feel as if you're in heaven. Various hiking trails begin from *Mount Cook Village*, at 750m, and, of course, there are planes and helicopters which fly you to Tasman Glacier above the mountain summit.

SIGHTSEEING

EDMUND HILLARY ALPINE CENTRE ☂

From the roof of New Zealand to the roof of the world: the 3-D cinema with small museum at the Hermitage Hotel in Mount Cook Village is dedicated to the expeditions of famous New Zealand mountaineer Sir Edmund Hillary. A 75-minute documentary is devoted to his ascent of Mount Everest, while the film *Mount Cook Magic* is all about the mountain where Hillary learned his mountaineering skills. *Daily 9am–4pm | NZ$20 | Terrace Road*

SPORT & ACTIVITIES

ALPS 2 OCEAN CYCLE TRAIL

The popular trail starts at Mount Cook and continues for six to eight days as far as Oamaru on the east coast. *alps2ocean.com*

HOOKER VALLEY TRACK

Wildflowers in front of the snow-covered mountains make a beautiful picture. But that's not the only photo opportunity along the route. The three-hour track through Hooker Valley in the direction of Mount Cook leads across several rope bridges, past the Mueller Glacier and ends at Hooker Lake where icebergs float. It starts off at White Horse Hill Campground at the end of Hooker Valley Road, 2km from Mount Cook Village.

TASMAN GLACIER LAKE CRUISE ★

Lumps of ice constantly break off the Tasman Glacier and float like gigantic ice cubes around Tasman Glacier Lake. On boat tours you approach the ice giant and the gorge of the glacier and you can try the 300 to 500-year-old ice crystals. If you want to save money: from the shore, the lake looks just as impressive. *2.5 hr incl. transfer from Mount Cook Village 10km away and 30-min hike | NZ$149 | tel. 03 435 1855 | glentanner.co.nz*

AROUND AORAKI/ MOUNT COOK

22 LAKE OHAU

90km/1 hr 15 mins from Mount Cook Village (car)

The best thing about Lake Ohau is the tranquillity. There are no jet skiers, paragliders or parachutists anywhere to be seen. You share the pebble beach with a few sandflies, and the nearby mountains look even more majestic when you swim towards them alone in the pale blue lake. On the lake shore there are several camping grounds for caravans with stunning views of the lake. *D14*

INSIDER TIP
Blue wonder

23 LAKE TEKAPO ★

105km/1 hr 10 mins from Mount Cook Village (car)

More touristy than Lake Ohau, but equally photogenic: Lake Tekapo gleams so bright blue that you have to squint when you look at it. And after the sun has set, the sky shines particularly brightly because Lake Tekapo is one of the places in the world where you can see the most stars. On *Mount John* above the lake is the *Observatory (times and prices depending on season, e.g. Summit Experience, 2 hr, approx. NZ$169 | signpost at SH 8 | earthandsky.co.nz)* which has New Zealand's biggest telescope. Nearby is the start of the wonderful *Summit Circuit Track (30–45 mins)* with panoramic vistas of the lake and the region's mountains. *D13–14*

FRANZ JOSEF

(*D13*) **Only three glaciers in the world reach as far as the rainforest. Perito Moreno Glacier is in Argentina, while the other two are on New Zealand's west coast where they join with gigantic ice flows and reach inland:** ★ **Franz Josef Glacier and the slightly smaller Fox Glacier, 25km further south.**

Nestled between mountain peaks

Explore the fascinating icy environment of Fox Glacier

and in the heart of the rainforest, the *Village* is 6km from the Franz Josef Glacier (named by the geologist Julius von Haast after the Austrian Emperor Franz Josef). There is plenty of accommodation here and you can book glacier tours with one of the tour operators.

SIGHTSEEING

WEST COAST WILDLIFE CENTRE

Seeing a kiwi in the wild is like drawing a lucky number in the lottery. *Rowi kiwis*, in particular, are extremely rare: only 400 individuals of this species still live in the wild. This breeding station works to ensure their survival. With a *Backstage Kiwi Pass* for NZ$60 (children NZ$24) you can even watch how kiwi chicks hatch from the eggs. *Daily 9am–3pm | NZ$32, children NZ$14 (pre-book online) | Cowan/corner of Cron Street | wildkiwi. co.nz*

EATING & DRINKING

SNAKE BITE BREWERY

Asian street food, chocolate cake and craft beer – here, dishes are served that don't necessarily go together, but somehow complement each other. The main thing is the culinary variety in the middle of the rainforest! *Mon– Sat 7.30am–8pm, Sun until 3pm | 28 Main Road | tel. 03 752 0234 | snakebite.co.nz | $*

SPORT & ACTIVITIES

GLACIER TOURS

Take a helicopter tour to the glacier, e.g. with *Franz Josef Glacier Guides (NZ$485 | franzjosefglacier.com)*, or

Beauty doubled: Mount Tasman and Mount Cook are reflected in Lake Matheson

go on a sightseeing flight over the glacier in a propeller aircraft, e.g. with *Air Safaris (NZ$425 | airsafaris.co.nz)*. Otherwise, you can hike to the glacier. The tour takes 45 minutes over a rocky riverbed to the viewpoint at the foot of the glacier. The trail begins at a car park five minutes by car from Franz Josef.

WELLNESS

WAIHO HOT TUBS

Relax in heated wooden hot tubs at the heart of the rainforest. Private hot tubs can be booked for an hour each for up to four people and are refilled with fresh water straight from a mountain stream after each visit. *Daily 2–9pm | 2 people NZ$89, children NZ$10 | 64 B Cron Street | tel. 03 752 0009 | waihohottubs.co.nz*

AROUND FRANZ JOSEF

24 FOX GLACIER ★

25km/30 mins from Franz Josef (car)
You can fly to the smaller glacier, Fox Glacier, by helicopter, e.g. with *Fox Glacier Guiding (NZ$499 | foxguides. co.nz)*, or walk over rocky boulders on the *Fox Glacier Walk* heading for the icy gorge. The tour *(1 hr)* starts at a car park 2km south of *Fox Glacier Township*. On the way, you have to jump across several small streams; at the end is an impressive viewing platform above the glacier. *▱ D13*

25 LAKE MATHESON

30km/30 mins from Franz Josef (car)
You will find a very popular photo opportunity south of Franz Josef. In

so clear that you can watch the fish under the surface from the canoe. On the lake shore is a *DOC campsite (doc. govt.nz)*. *C13*

HOKITIKA

(E12) **During the gold rush Hokitika was one of New Zealand's densely populated towns. Historic buildings and shops with Wild West façades are still reminders of that era.**

Today, in the town between the sea and the Alps everything is about the "green gold" – jade from the surrounding rivers. Numerous jewellery ateliers in Hokitika (pop. 4,000) make creative pieces with the stone.

fine weather, Mount Cook and Mount Tasman are reflected here in the "mirror lake" Lake Matheson. Enjoy this view on a 90-minute hike around the lake. *D13*

26 GILLESPIES BEACH
45km/1 hr from Franz Josef (car)
Salty spray flies in your face, while your back is turned on snow-covered summits. South-west of Franz Josef, you can build sculptures of driftwood, stack pebbles on top of each other or gaze at the foaming Tasman Sea. But don't forget the sandfly spray! *D13*

27 LAKE PARINGA
95km/1 hr 15 mins from Franz Josef (car)
More beautiful than a painting: when the sunshine reflects the surroundings in Lake Paringa, you will not be able to resist taking photos. The lake is

EATING & DRINKING

THE HOKITIKA SANDWICH COMPANY
Fresh from the oven: crusty sourdough sandwiches filled with locally sourced ingredients. Choose from organic beef pastrami, Southland cheese and west coast butter. Chase it down with a delicious fruit smoothie. *Tue–Sat 10am–2pm | 83 Revell Street | tel. 03 429 2019 | FB: The Hokitika Sandwich Company | $*

SHOPPING

BONZ 'N' STONZ
Design your own necklace charms from jade or bone and create your jewellery under expert instruction. The

courses last three to six hours and cost between NZ$100 and NZ$190. *Daily 9am–5pm | 16 Hamilton Street | tel. 03 755 6504 | bonz-n-stonz.co.nz*

TECTONIC JADE

Charms and artworks from especially rare jade stones, made using traditional methods. Each amulet has a different meaning and, according to the owner Rex Scott, is not made from stone but "tears of the earth". *Daily 8.30am–5pm | 67 Revell Street | tel. 03 755 6644 | tectonicjade.com*

FESTIVALS

WILDFOODS FESTIVAL

At the *Wildfoods Festival* in March, the population of Hokitika increases threefold as visitors flock to the town from across the country to try bush specialities such as worms and deep-fried beetles. *wildfoods.co.nz*

INSIDER TIP
Snack on bugs

A typical jade pendant

NIGHTLIFE

REGENT THEATRE ☂

If it's raining (which happens frequently on the west coast) why not visit this beautiful old cinema with red-cushioned seats in an art deco building from 1935? *Daily | 23 Weld Street | tel. 03 755 8101 | hokitika regent.com*

WOODSTOCK HOTEL

The first gold-diggers were already getting drunk in this pub and hotel in 1870. Nowadays, regular live bands perform here. At the jam session on Sunday everyone is allowed on stage – locals and tourists. The view from the beer garden over the mountains and rivers is spectacular. You should definitely try the fish & chips! *Daily from 4pm | 250 Woodstock Rimu Road | tel. 03 755 8909 | woodstock hotel.net | $*

AROUND HOKITIKA

⁲⁸ LAKE MAHINAPUA

11km/10 mins from Hokitika (car)
At last, a lake on the west coast where you don't shiver with cold. Jump from the long boardwalk into the water,

which is a pleasant temperature, and swim towards the snow-covered Alps in the distance! It's worth spending a night on the *DOC Campsite (doc.govt. nz)* by the lakeside if only to watch the fiery red sunsets. *E12*

☺ ROSS ☻

25km/20 mins from Hokitika (car)

The biggest gold nugget ever to be found in New Zealand (2.8kg!) was from Ross, south-west of Hokitika. It's

INSIDER TIP
Dig for gold

an incentive to borrow the gold-mining tools at the Ross Goldfields Information & Heritage Centre *(4 Aylmer Street | tel. 03 755 4077 | ross-goldtown.org)* and try your luck at Jones Creek. *E12*

☒ HOKITIKA GORGE

30km/30 mins from Hokitika (car)

No photoshopping here! The water in the glacial river really is as turquoise as it looks in the photos! You can see it for yourself. From the car park it's a 15-minute walk to the rope bridge over the gorge. Unfortunately, there are lots of sandflies. *E12*

GREYMOUTH

(E12) **In Greymouth, the biggest town on the west coast (pop. 10,000), there used to be 47 hotels – today, there are only six. Since the wood and coal industry moved away, the building façades are crumbling, and the number of residents is in decline.**

Monteiths Brewery in Greymouth dates back to the gold rush era

The rather functional town at the mouth of the Grey River is not so much a tourist destination as a starting point for trips along the wild west coast with its windswept beaches and towns full of eccentric hippie characters. The coast extends for 500km along the stormy Tasman Sea from Westport in the north to the Haast Pass in the south: a unique mix of rainforests, glaciers, sea and snow-covered summits that feels almost unreal.

EATING & DRINKING

MONTEITHS BREWERY

What does the west coast taste like? Like burgers and beer from Monteiths!

You can taste both in the brewery's restaurant – and during guided tours *(daily 4pm, NZ$35)* find out all about the history of the 150-year-old beer. *Mon–Thu 3–9pm, Wed–Sun 11am–9pm | 60 Herbert Street | tel. 03 768 4149 | thebrewery.co.nz | $*

SPORT & ACTIVITIES

WEST COAST WILDERNESS TRAIL

The bike trail leads from Greymouth 139km through rainforests and along secluded lakes and empty beaches filled with driftwood. It's best to book accommodation in advance along the route in *Kumara* and *Hokitika*. The Trail Shuttle Service from *West Coast Wilderness (trailtransport.co.nz)* rents bikes, transports luggage and collects it en route, if you prefer not to continue along the entire trail.

AROUND GREYMOUTH

31 SHANTYTOWN 👾

10km/10 mins from Greymouth (car)
Enjoy a nostalgia trip back to the year 1860. In the reconstructed gold-rush town, children can wash gold, travel on a steam locomotive through the rainforest or have their photos taken in historic costumes. *Daily 9am–4pm | adults NZ$36, children over 5 years NZ$18.50 | 316 Rutherglen Road | www.shantytown.co.nz | ⊙ 3 hrs | ⊞ E12*

32 PUNAKAIKI

45km/40 mins from Greymouth (car)
It took a long time to stack all those pancakes on top of each other: the *Pancake Rocks* at Tasman Bay in Punakaiki are estimated to be about 30 million years old. A magnificent photo backdrop – especially when the spray rushes through the holes in the rocks. The picturesque *Punakaiki Beach Camp (5 Owen Street | tel. 03 731 1894 | punakaikibeachcamp.co.nz | $–$$)* is between the beach, rainforest and tall cliffs and has space for camper vans and tents. There are also huts and reasonably priced holiday houses. You can explore more of the wilderness on *Canoe Tours (river kayaking.co.nz)* on the Pororari River. ⊞ E11

33 NORTHERN WEST COAST & WESTPORT

100km/1 hr 30 mins from Greymouth to Westport (car)
The sleepy town of Westport (pop. 4,000) is the gateway to the secluded northern part of the west coast. *Tauranga Bay*, 12km along the coast, is a popular meeting point for surfers and seals. You will feel very remote in the village of *Karamea*, which, with its subtropical microclimate, lies between the mountains and sea 90km further north on the edge of Kahurangi National Park. Under Nikau palms in the dense rainforest you can stay overnight in the pleasant cottages or comfortable double rooms of *Last Resort (26 rooms | 71 Waverley Street | tel. 03 782 6617 | lastresortkaramea. co.nz | $)* which has an excellent

Both roses and artists thrive in Nelson's mild climate

restaurant. Nearby, there are karst caves and the start of the *Heaphy Track*, one of New Zealand's Great Walks, in Kahurangi National Park. The warm climate also benefits *Mokihinui*, 50km north of Westport. Here you can camp at the mouth of the Mokihinui River which is excellent for swimming and canoeing. Also highly recommended is the *Cowshed Café (298 De Malmanches Road | $)* where the wood-fired pizza oven is fuelled by driftwood from the beach. 🛏 *E–F10–11*

34 REEFTON 👯

80km/1 hr from Greymouth (car)

INSIDER TIP
Going for gold

In the town of Reefton (pop. 1,000), 150 years after the gold rush, you can still see rugged characters with dirty boots in old gold-miners' huts brewing tea in tin billy cans over an open fire. At the *Bearded Mining Company (admission for a donation |*

37 Walsh Street | tel. 03 732 8377 | reefton.co.nz | ⏱ 1 hr) you can learn gold panning. 🛏 *F11*

NELSON

(🛏 *G10*) **A small town with big ideas. In Nelson (pop. 50,000) you can explore the cultural landscape between Abel Tasman National Park and Marlborough Sounds.**

About 400 artists live in the town which boasts more hours of sunshine that anywhere else in New Zealand. The artists exhibit their works in museums and galleries, e.g. *The Suter Art Gallery (daily 9.30am–4.30pm | free admission | 208 Bridge Street | thesuter.org.nz | ⏱ 30 mins)*. The *Wow Museum* shows cool "art on the body". What else? The town has plenty of beautiful old wooden villas and regular markets.

SIGHTSEEING

WORLD OF WEARABLE ART (WOW)

It's retro and futuristic at the same time. The museum displays vintage cars and "wearable art" that looks as if the Icelandic singer and performance-art artist Björk commissioned the Wow to design stage outfits for her. Every year new pieces are added from the design competition "World of Wearable Art" (WOW). And every September, fashion and costume designers from around the world can test their creative talents. *Daily 10am–5pm | NZ$24 | 95 Quarantine Road | worldofwearableart.com | ⏱ 1.5 hrs*

PARKER GALLERY

Kiwi art: paintings, sculptures, jewellery and photography by artists from Nelson and around. *Mon–Fri 9.30am–4.30pm, Sat 10am–4pm | 90 Achilles Av. | parkergallery.nz | ⏱ 30 mins*

EATING & DRINKING

THE KITCHEN

Superfood smoothies, halloumi salad and organic cappuccinos: in the bright restaurant with purist furniture it's all about *positive eating*. All ingredients come from the region and are 100 % organic. There are vegan banana waffles with raspberry chia jam for breakfast and quinoa salads or paleo burgers with manuka bacon and organic beef for lunch. *Mon–Sat 8am–2.30pm | 111 Bridge Street | tel. 021 195 8246 | ktchn.co.nz | $$$*

SHOPPING

JENS HANSEN

There it is – the ring everyone is looking for! Jens Hansen, a Danish-born jewellery designer, created the famous magic ring from *The Lord of the Rings*. Since

INSIDER TIP **The real Lord of the Rings!**

The stunning beaches in Abel Tasman National Park are only accessible on foot or by boat

his death in 1999, his son has continued the business and also sells models, which were inspired by actors from the film: "The Ring for Viggo" or "The Ring for Cate". *Mon–Fri 9am–5pm, Sat 9am–2pm | 320 Trafalgar Square | jenshansen.com*

MARKETS

Every Wednesday at the *Farmer's Market (8am–1pm | Maitai Blvd)* there are fresh figs and apples from the vicinity. Live bands perform. On Saturdays, people meet at *Nelson Market (8am–1pm)* between artisan products and local nectarines at *Montgomery Square* and on Sundays at the *Flea Market (8am–1pm)* at the same location.

BEACHES

The best swimming locations are on the outskirts of the city at *Tahunanui Beach* or on *Rabbit Island* with *glamping sites (from SH 60, turn off to Upper Moutere | applebyhouse.co.nz).*

NIGHTLIFE

THE WORKSHOP

A café, bar and micro-brewery in an old workshop. The bar, in an old ship's container with a car on the roof, has alternative rock bands, swing dance evenings and serves draught craft beer. Tasty snacks include burgers, steaks and fish dishes. *Wed–Sun 3–11pm | 32c New Street | tel. 021 556 158 | the workshopbrewery.co.nz | $*

AROUND NELSON

35 ABEL TASMAN NATIONAL PARK ★

60km/1 hr from Nelson to Marahau or 125km/2 hrs 30 mins to Totaranui (car)

Turquoise gleaming water the right temperature for swimming (!) and golden beaches nestled in thick vegetation – it's no wonder that New Zealand's smallest national park north-west of Nelson attracts crowds of visitors. A good starting point is the *campsite at Totaranui (end Dec–start Feb minimum 3 days | book online at doc.govt.nz | $)* at the north end of the national park. After sunset, the only light is from the moon and torches. Conversations with your neighbours revolve around the size of the fish that were caught by the cliffs during the day. What could be more idyllic?

On the *Abel Tasman Coastal Track*, which leads 60km from Totaranui to Marahau, you can hike in four or five days from one dream beach to the next. Or enjoy a comfortable ride in the *water taxi (approx. NZ$50 | tel. 03 527 8083 | aqua taxi.co.nz)* and ask to be dropped off at a beach of your choice and to be collected in the evening. From Torrent Bay, halfway along the route, a path leads through the rainforest to the cliff pool with emerald-green water.

> **INSIDER TIP**
> **Slip and slide in the rainforest**

On a 10-m-long rock-slide, you can slide into *Cleopatra's Pool*.

If you don't want to hike, *Marahau Sea Kayaks (kayak for 2 people approx. NZ$210/day | 10 Franklin Street | tel. 0800 529 257 | msk.co.nz)* hires kayaks for trips along the coast and organizes one- or multi-day tours with a guide. The area's most beautiful beach is surely the long, crescent-shaped 🎋 *Kaiteriteri Beach* with gleaming white sand. 🗺 *G10*

🔢 GOLDEN BAY

125km/2 hrs from Nelson to Collingwood (car)

The *Farewell Spit* in the far north-west is South Island's happy ending. The narrow headland measures 35km and embraces Golden Bay from the left. Four kilometres are open to the public, while the rest of the nature reserve is filled with migratory birds, sea lions and windswept dunes that are only accessible as part of guided tours, e.g. with *Farewell Spit Eco Tours (6.5 hrs/ NZ$165 | from Collingwood | farewellspit.com)*. Also fabulous is a horse ride through the salty spray at Puponga Beach at the foot of Farewell Spit – tours for beginners with *Cape Farewell Horse Treks (1.5 hr/ NZ$100 | from Collingwood | horsetreksnz.co. nz)*. The best swimming beaches in Golden Bay are *Pohara*, *Tata Beach* and *Totaranui* at the start of the Abel Tasman National Park. 🎋 *Wharariki Beach* is not suitable for swimming, but it's dramatic and beautiful and is located on the west coast near Puponga *(20 mins on foot from the car park)* with waves splashing around cliff arches out in the sea. On the *Wainui Falls Track* near Mohua it's a 40-minute walk to a waterfall in the rainforest. At *The Mussel Inn (mussel inn.co.nz)* between the hippie towns of Collingwood and Takaka, in the middle of nowhere, you might just experience the party night of your life.

Explore dramatic Whariki Beach on horseback for a new perspective

INSIDER TIP
The hut life Kiwi style

Musicians from all over New Zealand perform in the rustic hut with disco ball on the ceiling in the small coastal community of Onekaka. A rebellious café, which has been brewing its own beer since the 1990s, organizes open-mic evenings and serves fresh seafood (you should definitely try the green-lipped mussels!). ⏎ *F–G 9–10*

37 KAHURANGI NATIONAL PARK
155km/2 hrs 30 mins from Nelson to Brown Hut/starting point for Heaphy Track (car)

The *Heaphy Track*, one of New Zealand's Great Walks, continues for 78km through subtropical rainforest, river valleys and secluded beaches. The Kahurangi *(doc.govt.nz)*, New Zealand's second largest national park to the east of Nelson, is known as "valuable treasure" in Maori language, because it leads to the west coast with its many rivers filled with *pounamu* (greenstone). The chattering of tuis and bellbirds fills the air and occasionally large kiwis rustle in the bush. If you feel confident, in *Mount Owen* there is a labyrinthine cave system. ⏎ *F10*

38 NELSON LAKES NATIONAL PARK
80km/1 hr 10 mins from Nelson to St Arnaud (car)

South of Nelson, glaciers were at work shaping the unique landscape with steep mountains and large lakes. A good starting point for hikes is the village of *St Arnaud* on Lake Rotoiti. If you are a keen angler, the lakes in the park are full of trout. The nearby *Rainbow Ski Field* is open from June to October. ⏎ *F–G11*

DISCOVERY TOURS

Do you want to get under the skin of the country? Then our discovery tours provide the perfect guide – they include advice on which sights to visit, tips on where to stop for that perfect holiday snap, a choice of the best places to eat and drink, and suggestions for fun activities.

❶ NEW ZEALAND AT A GLANCE

- ➤ Dive with dolphins in the turquoise water
- ➤ Dig for hot springs at the beach
- ➤ Hike like Frodo through landscapes straight out of *Lord of the Rings*

📍 Auckland		Christchurch
→ 3,600km	🚗	23 days (54 hrs driving time)

ⓘ Cost: approx. NZ$12,500 for two people (all incl.)
Many roads are narrow and full of bends; travel times are often longer than planned. The flight from ㉖ **Queenstown** to **Milford Sound** is weather dependent *(from NZ$349 | 1 hr | milfordflights.co.nz)*.

Auckland is known as the "City of Sails" for good reason

GAZE DOWN ON THE CITY

You're ready to set off in ① Auckland ➤ p. 50. Walk along the waterfront to the restaurants and cafés at Viaduct Harbour and in the evening survey the city's sea of lights from the Sky Tower. In the morning, enjoy breakfast at Café Dizengoff *(daily 6.30am–4pm | 256 Ponsonby Road | tel. 09 360 0108 | $)* in the trendy district of Ponsonby and stroll around the area's boutiques and second-hand shops. In the afternoon, there is still time to view contemporary art in the Auckland Art Gallery *(daily 10am–5pm | NZ$20 | Wellesley Street E | aucklandartgallery.com)*, New Zealand's largest with its impressive atrium made of kauri wood.

IN THE BEAUTIFUL BAY OF THE NORTH

Head for the sea! *In the north, past Auckland,* the traffic gets lighter and the dream beaches of *Tutukaka Coast* come into view. Stop for a swim on the golden beach at ② Matapouri Bay and continue to the Bay of Islands. In the early evening arrive at the small coastal town of ③ Russell ➤ p. 46 and check in for two nights at the Duke of Marlborough *(theduke.co.nz)* – a white wooden villa with colonial charm and a sea view. The next day, explore the most beautiful bays in the Bay of Islands on a

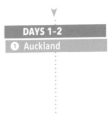

DAYS 1–2
① Auckland

DAYS 3–4

201km
② Matapouri Bay

87km
③ Russell

half-day boat tour *(NZ$135 | tel. 0800 653 339 | dolphin cruises.co.nz)* and go swimming with the dolphins.

DAYS 5–6

74km

❹ Waitangi Treaty Grounds

120km

❺ Waipoua Kauri Forest

35km

❻ Oponomi Hotel

BACK TO WHERE IT ALL BEGAN

The first stop of the day is at the ❹ Waitangi Treaty Grounds ➤ p. 46. Afterwards, *drive to* ❺ Waipoua Kauri Forest ➤ p. 49 *on the west coast*. Here, Tane Mahuta, a kauri tree 51m tall, soars above the forest. The tree is over 2,000 years old. Stop overnight at the ❻ Oponomi Hotel *(opononihotel.com)* in Omapere at Hokianga Harbour with a view of the gigantic dunes of Rangi Point. In the morning, *head back southwards* to the Hauraki Gulf, where you can spend the rest of the day on the beautiful ❼ Pakiri Beach. In the evening, head for the ❽ Sawmill Café *(142 Pakiri Road | tel. 09 4 22 60 19 | sawmillcafe.co.nz | $)* $) in the nearby surfer town of Leigh. Later in the evening, after you've enjoyed a quiet dinner (e.g. shoulder of lamb or octopus), local bands take over the stage. Then, simply fall into bed here – the restaurant also offers rooms.

PENINSULA FULL OF BEACHES
Carry on to the ❾ Coromandel Peninsula ➤ p. 57. First, stop in the old gold-rush location of Coromandel Town at the Oyster Company *(daily 9am–4.30pm | 1611 Manaia Road | freshoysters.co.nz | $)*, a wooden shack by the sea, where you can get fresh oysters. The beach at Hahei with its turquoise-blue sea is really beautiful. Stay here at Tatahi Lodge *(tatahilodge.co.nz)*), which has a subtropical garden. In the morning, set off on a kayak tour from the beach *(3 hrs | NZ$125 | kayaktours.co.nz)* to the cliff caves of Cathedral Cove and then dig on Hot Water Beach for the hot springs (bring a spade!). If you don't like crowded beaches, carry on to the wild bay of Opoutere Beach and enjoy a wonderful picnic hidden away in the dunes behind a pine forest. Stay the night at the popular surfer spot Whangamata, where seagulls steal chips off your plate at the numerous cafés along Port Road. You can book a board and surfing course along with your room at the Surf N Stay *(surfnstaynew zealand.com)* hotel near the wide beach full of spray.

INSIDER TIP
Hidden-away beach

AT THE HEART OF MAORI CULTURE
First thing in the morning, head for ❿ Mount Maunganui ➤ p. 66 and climb the mountain with a panoramic view of the ocean (approx. 45 min). Then, enjoy a refreshing swim in the sea and lunch on the waterfront. In the late afternoon you arrive at the steaming thermal region of ⓫ Rotorua ➤ p. 61. In the Maori village of Te Puia you can watch the steaming springs after sunset on the Geyser by night experience *(Wed– Sun 9–11pm | NZ$60 | Hemo Road | tel. 07 348 9047 |*

210km
❼ Pakiri Beach

12km
❽ Sawmill Café

DAYS 7–8
208km
❾ Coromandel Peninsula

DAYS 9–10
273km
❿ Mount Maunganui

75km
⓫ Rotorua

tepuia.com) and hike through typical New Zealand bush. Next day, avoid the expensive thermal baths on your left and drive to ⑫ Kerosene Creek, *around 30km south.* This river has warm water and is in the middle of the forest! Now, get ready for the tour's longest stretch in the car. But don't worry, it's definitely not boring because *the route to Wellington* passes through wonderful fantasy film landscapes, *along Desert Road and past Tongariro National Park* with snow-covered volcanic summits and *on the SH1 along the beautiful Kapiti Coast.* In the evening, you arrive in ⑬ Wellington ➤ p. 80.

28km
⑫ Kerosene Creek

468km

⑬ Wellington

INSIDER TIP
Hot enough for a bath

DAYS 11–12

CROSS INTO THE RUGGED SOUTH

Baristas are the new DJs – at least they are in New Zealand's coffee capital. Start the day with a flat white or cold brew in one of the more than 300 cafés, for example The Hangar *(Mon–Fri 7am–3pm, Sat/Sun 8am–3pm | 119 Dixon Street | hangarcafe.co.nz).* In the cable car, travel to the Botanic Gardens *above the city* for a spectacular panoramic view over Wellington and then stroll back to the centre. From Cuba Street, New Zealand's reputedly coolest street, with its numerous art galleries, shops and graffitied walls, it's only a few steps to the interactive Te Papa Tongarewa, where every item on display defines New Zealand's heritage, including Maori canoes, simulated earthquakes and Moa bones. In the late afternoon, *catch the ferry to South Island* and enjoy the view of the Marlborough Sounds when the sunset bathes the coastal landscape in deep orange hues. *From the ferry wharf in* Picton ➤ p. 90 *carry on by boat to* ⑭ The Portage Hotel *(theportage.co.nz),* which is situated among beautiful dense green vegetation on Kenepuru Sound. Wake up with a view of the bright blue sparkling sea and spend a day exploring in kayaks.

119km
⑭ The Portage Hotel

DAYS 13–16
144km
⑮ Nelson
140km

PLAY GOLD PROSPECTOR ON THE WEST COAST

In the morning, *the boat takes you back to Picton. You can get in your hire car again and explore* ⑮ Nelson ➤ p. 129, *before heading for the sparsely populated*

Pause in Picton – with a view of the water

west coast. Wind your way through ⑯ Buller Gorge, where you can walk across New Zealand's longest swing bridge. In the early afternoon, you arrive at Punakaiki ➤ p. 128. The main attraction here are the ⑰ Pancake Rocks where the wild Tasman Bay bubbles up. In the rainforest behind the beach in Te Miko are the wonderful wooden cottages of the ⑱ Te Nikau Retreats *(tenikauretreat.co.nz)*. On one of the most spectacular coast roads in the world, next day you *head further south.* If you are travelling with children, at Shantytown ➤ p. 128 near Greymouth you can stop off and soak up the gold-rush atmosphere. Otherwise, continue to ⑲ Hokitika ➤ p. 125. Here, it's all about the *greenstone* because the rivers near the town are rich in jade. At Bonz 'n' Stonz you can even design and polish a lucky charm. In the early evening, the ⑳ Franz Josef Glacier ➤ p. 122 finally comes into view with its massive ice flows. Spend the night surrounded by the dense rainforest at the Scenic Hotel Franz Josef Glacier *(scenichotelgroup.co.nz)*, with a view of the snow-covered mountains. Early next morning it's time

⑯ Buller Gorge

127km

⑰ Pancake Rocks

4km

⑱ Te Nikau Retreats

92km

⑲ Hokitika

134km

⑳ Franz Josef Glacier

for your Heli-Hike *(NZ$485 | helicopter.co.nz)* to the glacier; this involves clambering through the unique ice landscape for two hours with a mountain guide. *Before continuing inland next day to the Haast Pass,* you should definitely stop to take photos at the crystal-clear ㉑ Lake Paringa ➤ p. 125, where the mountains and forests are reflected in the water! In the early evening you arrive at the ㉒ Blue Pools in a rock gorge with bright blue glacier water. Jump into the ice-cold water and then fall into a deep sleep in the nearby ㉓ Mountain View Makarora *(makarora.com)* at the heart of Mount Aspiring National Park ➤ p. 120.

WINE GEEKS & ADRENALIN JUNKIES

These mountains separate worlds. If the stormy weather on the west coast made it necessary to wear a fleece, in the morning in ㉔ Wanaka ➤ p. 118 in Central Otago it is probably warm and sunny. Relax for a couple of days in the many bays of Lake Wanaka with a view of Mount Aspiring. If you're hiking, enjoy the magnificent countryside and the Pinot Noir at Rippon

A vineyard with a view this good must produce decent wine: Rippon Vineyard on Lake Wanaka

Vineyard, or stretch your legs on a bike tour along the lake. In the morning, *continue south on a road over a winding pass* towards hectic Queenstown. On the way, you can enjoy a pleasant meal in the restaurant of the atmospheric ㉕ Cardrona Hotels *(daily 9am–10pm | 2312 Cardrona Valley Road | tel. 03 443 8153 | cardrona hotel.co.nz | $$)*, which dates back to the gold-rush era. In ㉖ Queenstown ➤ p. 114 you will be amazed how touristy New Zealand can be. Get your adrenalin shot from river rafting, bungy jumping or paragliding – or take in the magnificent mountain scenery on a peaceful hike or bike tour. When Queenstown fades in the dimmed light of night, it's time for a pub crawl. Excellent live bands play e.g. at the Sherwood Hotel *(554 Frankton Road | sherwoodqueens town.nz | $$)* with cocktail bar, where you can also enjoy healthy and nutritious meals. You should plan a half day for ㉗ Glenorchy ➤ p. 120. Here, the boundaries are blurred between cinema and reality because so many *Lord of the Rings* scenes were filmed around town.

DAYS 19–20

31km

㉕ Cardrona Hotels

40km

㉖ Queenstown

50km

㉗ Glenorchy

BLUE WONDERS & THE WILD WEST

In the morning, if you *turn off the SH8 to Lake Ohau* you will be one of the only cars on the road, as most tourists carry on to Lake Pukaki or Lake Tekapo. ㉘ Lake Ohau sparkles just as wonderfully blue – and you can enjoy it all to yourself. In the region's only accommodation at Lake Ohau Lodge *(ohau.co.nz)* above the lake you will meet (at the very most) a few cyclists who are on the *Alps 2 Ocean Trail*. Despite the view of Mount Cook, the rooms are not overpriced. If you like swimming in mountain rivers, then you will love ㉙ Geraldine in the heart of South Canterbury. Around the small town (pop. 3,500) at the foot of the Alps there are plenty of good swimming spots such as Te Moana (with waterfall!) in the middle of an impressive Wild West landscape. Twenty minutes by car outside the town you can stay overnight at the Waikonini Homestead *(waikonini homestead.co.nz)*, a B & B in a historic wooden villa on the edge of Peel Forest.

FINISH UP IN THE NEW, OLD CITY

In ㉚ Christchurch ➤ p. 93, discover how the city is reinventing itself with creative ideas after the earthquake in 2011. In recent years, some of the world's greatest street artists *(Street Art Walking Tours with Watch This Space | NZ$30 | tel.021 113 8502 | watch-thisspace.org.nz)* have created giant murals in what was the almost completely destroyed city centre. Smash Palace *(172 High Street | thesmashpalace.co.nz)* is a bar made from old buses and containers and there is even a Cardboard Cathedral *(234 Hereford Street)*. In the early evening, Cassels Brewery *(3 Garlands Road | tel. 03 3 89 53 59 | casselsbrewery.co.nz | $)* is worth a visit for its pizzas and craft beer – it's in The Tannery, a restored Victorian tannery full of boutiques and cafés in the district of Woolston. Check into your room at the Eco Villa *(ecovilla.co.nz)* with outdoor tubs in the garden. You can relax here in the dark in the warm water and take a last look at the Southern Cross.

② GREAT BARRIER ISLAND – DISCOVER THE ECO-ISLE

➤ Walk barefoot through the rainforest
➤ Watch the starry sky twinkle, free from light pollution
➤ Bathe in warm thermal springs in the bush

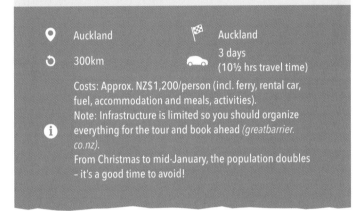

📍 Auckland   🏁 Auckland

🔄 300km   🚗 3 days (10½ hrs travel time)

ℹ️ Costs: Approx. NZ$1,200/person (incl. ferry, rental car, fuel, accommodation and meals, activities).
Note: Infrastructure is limited so you should organize everything for the tour and book ahead *(greatbarrier. co.nz)*.
From Christmas to mid-January, the population doubles – it's a good time to avoid!

WALKING THERAPY & STAR WELLNESS

From the Sealink ferry terminal *(sealink.co.nz)* in the Wynyard Quarter in ❶ Auckland ➤ p. 50 *the ferry takes you early morning on a 4.5-hour tour through the Hauraki Gulf to* ❷ Tryphena, the main town on Great Barrier. Hire car companies come to the harbour. Shoal Bay Pottery *(Shoal Bay Road)* is the first port of call and is about three minutes from the terminal; it has beautiful handcrafted ceramics and beach art. Head to Stonewall Village for a snack – this is Tryphena's mini-centre with the largest of the island's three shops and a few restaurants. Pa Beach Café is pleasant. Then, head for ❸ Medlands Beach Lodge. The town on the long beach is *10 minutes away on the eastern side of the island.* You'll find sand, waves and a few holiday houses – an idyllic retreat. Check in for two nights at Medlands Beach Lodge *(medlandsbeachlodge.com)*, a pleasant B&B with beach views. Vicky from the Waiora Beach Retreat *(53 Sandhills Road | tel. 09 4 29 01 29 | waiorabeachretreat.nz)* helps you during the three-hour

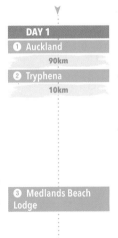

DAY 1
❶ Auckland
90km
❷ Tryphena
10km

❸ Medlands Beach Lodge

Nature Forest Therapy Walk *(NZ$75)* to use all your senses and go barefoot to explore Medland's nature. After dark, count shooting stars with the star guides from Good Heavens *(NZ$90 | Medlands Beach | tel. 09 429 0876 | goodheavens.co.nz).* Since 2017, Barrier Island is one of three Dark Sky Sanctuaries worldwide; away from any light pollution you can hardly see the sky for the stars. That's thanks to the giant telescope.

CLIMB THE WINDY CANYON

Start the day with a swim, go surfing or enjoy a walk on Medlands Beach, *then head for the lonely north.* You can stock up with supplies on the way in ④ Claris, where there is a shop and the café My Fat Puku *(FB: myfatpuku)* for a good coffee break. *Turn right onto Gray Road and after 10 minutes you arrive at* ⑤ Awana Bay, another dream bay for swimming and relaxation. Then continue to the starting point of a 15-minute short walk to ⑥ Windy Canyon. *Drive slowly or you will miss the sign on the left-hand side!* Steps lead into the gorge surrounded by steep rock faces swept by the wind. *Carry on until you see the spectacular view! Then, continue driving as far as* ⑦ Port Fitzroy, a beautiful, protected natural harbour with the island's third shop. It's worth booking a guided tour for the walk through Glenfern Sanctuary *(NZ$50 | Glenfern Road | tel. 09 429 0091),* a reserve with local plants and birds. You should book in advance! In the evening *return along the same route to* ⑧ Medlands Beach Lodge.

FROM BOARD TO BUSH

On the last day, head for ⑨ Whangaparapara and explore the west coast on a stand-up paddle board, which you can hire from Shiny Paua Stand *(NZ$25/hr | tel. 09 429 0603).* Then, on the quay, visit the old whaling station which has

The route up to Windy Canyon is steep, but worth the effort for the views

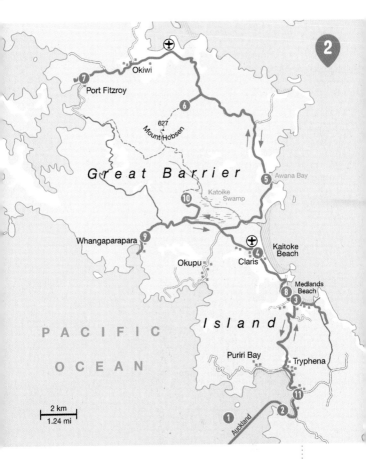

information about New Zealand's inglorious whaling era. *Take the same road back. After 3.5km on the left is the start of the 45-minute* bush hike *to the* ⑩ Kaitoke Hot Springs, *natural thermal springs in the middle of the bush. Take swimwear with you! Then, drive back about 40 minutes to* ⑪ Tryphena. *At 3pm the ferry departs for* ❶ Auckland. *Check-in is at 2pm and you arrive in the* Wynyard Quarter *at about 7.30pm, perfect timing for dinner in the trendy harbour quarter.*

DAY 3
14km
⑨ Whangaparapara
9km
⑩ Kaitoke Hot Springs
19km
⑪ Tryphena
92km
❶ Auckland

❸ ART DECO & WINE – CYCLING AROUND NAPIER

➤ Lose yourself in the art deco era
➤ Discover wineries by bike
➤ Feed penguins and marvel at rays

📍 Napier City Bike Hire

🏁 Napier City Bike Hire

🔄 36km

🚴 4–6 hrs
(2 hrs cycling time)

ℹ️ Costs: About NZ\$120/person incl. bike hire, lunch, admission.
Book your bike in advance from ❶ **Napier City Bike Hire** *(117 Marine Parade | tel. 0800 24 53 44 | bike-hirenapier.co.nz)* opposite the i-Site with flexible pick-up/drop-off times. Most of the route is signposted as the *Napier City Loop* with white route markers. Download the App Napier Art Deco beforehand with details of the architecture.
Reserve at table at the ❾ **Mission Estate**, (tel. 06 845 9354).

❶ Napier City Bike Hire

0.5km

❷ ASB Bank

0.2km

❸ Daily Telegraph Building

0.1km

❹ Art déco Shop

0.5km

BANKS, HUTS & MERMAIDS

Collect your bike from ❶ Napier City Bike Hire *on Marine Parade opposite the i-Site*. To start with, take a quick tour of the city. The app *Napier Art déco* informs you about the most important buildings. *Cross over the street and cycle in a southerly direction for a while, then turn right into Albion Street and right again into Hastings Street. After about 200m you will see the* ❷ ASB Bank – the first impressive historic building. Head inside and look upwards: a unique mixture of Maori symbols and art deco decorates the ceiling. *Then, turn left into Tennyson Street.* Stop to take photos at the ❸ Daily Telegraph Building. Turn around almost at the end of Tennyson Street and pass the attractive Masonic Hotel, before you look in the ❹ Art déco Shop *(daily 9am–5pm | 7 Tennyson Street)* opposite and admire the art deco collection of knick-knacks, hats and books. *Cross the Marine Parade, then turn left on a wonderful cycle route along the waterside, past* 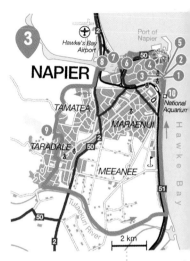 ⑤ Pania of the Reef, the sculpture of a Maori mermaid. *From here, simply follow the signs for the Napier City Loop,* cycle through the busy harbour district of Ahuriri where after 4km you can stop for coffee in the original ⑥ Shed 2 *(1 Lever Street | shed2.co.nz).*

WELCOME SIGHTS FOR BIRDWATCHERS

Follow the cycle route over the bridge, head through the wetland with many local birds, which you can watch from two ⑦ birdwatching points. *Then, turn around and head left onto Embankment Road and head straight on to the Ahuriri Estuary Walk,* past an ⑧ information board with interesting facts about the 1931 earthquake. The landscape becomes more rural: on the left are fields and on the right the canal. After a while the first vineyards come into view, and so you don't fall off the saddle, treat yourself to a light snack accompanied by an excellent wine in the pleasant ⑨ Mission Estate *(198 Church Street | missionestate.co.nz | $$).*

Continue on the Napier City Trail through the heart of the rural small town. Now, you will make some progress. In Riverside Park, *you head through green river meadows along the Tutaekuri River and endless vines until you arrive at the sea again* where Cape Kidnappers ➤ p. 76 and its white sandstone cliffs glint in the distance. With a bit of luck a tail wind will help you along the waterside to the ⑩ New Zealand National Aquarium *(daily 9am–5pm | NZ$24, children NZ$12 | 546 Marine Parade | nationalaquarium.co.nz),* where you can feed penguins and see sharks. From here, *continue straight ahead by the sea* and you will quickly arrive at your staring point at ① Napier City Bike Hire where you can hand back the bikes.

⑤ Pania of the Reef
4.3km
⑥ Shed 2
1.5km
⑦ Birdwatching points
0.8km
⑧ Information board
7km
⑨ Mission Estate
20km
⑩ New Zealand National Aquarium
1.2km
① Napier City Bike Hire

④ WILDLIFE TOUR THROUGH THE CATLINS

➤ Watch penguins jump out of the sea
➤ Surf with Hector's dolphins
➤ Bask on dreamy, deserted beaches

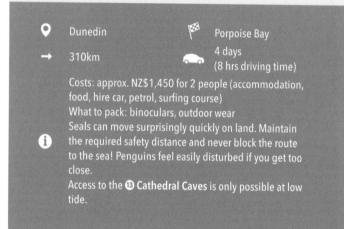

📍 Dunedin

🏁 Porpoise Bay

→ 310km

🚗 4 days
(8 hrs driving time)

Costs: approx. NZ$1,450 for 2 people (accommodation, food, hire car, petrol, surfing course)
What to pack: binoculars, outdoor wear
ℹ Seals can move surprisingly quickly on land. Maintain the required safety distance and never block the route to the sea! Penguins feel easily disturbed if you get too close.
Access to the ⑱ **Cathedral Caves** is only possible at low tide.

DAY 1
❶ Dunedin
100km
❷ Kaka Point
9km
❸ Roaring Bay
8km
❹ Kaka Point

ROARING BAYS & WILD BEACHES

From ❶ Dunedin ➤ p. 99 *head south*. In the early afternoon, you reach the coastal town of ❷ Kaka Point. Check into your crib (as the Kiwis call their simple, reasonably priced holiday homes) for two nights, e.g. Campbell Reef Cottage *(kakapointholidayhomes. co.nz)* or Nugget Lodge *(nuggetlodge.co.nz)* by the sea or on the cliffs by the beach. Then, make a detour to ❸ Roaring Bay *a little further south*. From shelters you can observe yellow-eyed penguins that hop out of the sea onto the shore at twilight. Tip: Find out about the current tides by phoning the Catlins Info Center *(tel. 03 415 8371 | catlins.org.nz)*. Back in ❹ Kaka Point there is fish & chips with freshly caught blue cod at The Point Café *(daily 9am–6pm | 58 Esplanade)*. Take your food to the beach and eat it at one of the wooden tables.

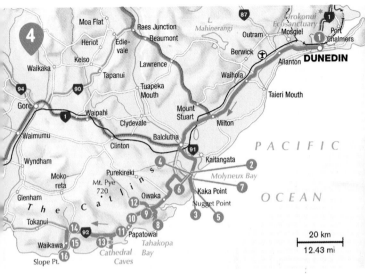

SEALS BELOW, ALBATROSSES ABOVE

Next morning, hike along the cliffs to the ⑤ lighthouse at Nugget Point and look down on the rocks (nuggets) dotted in the sea and the seal colony with over 500 animals. If you're lucky, albatrosses soar above your head, or rare elephant seals emerge out the sea. Enjoy the rest of your day on the beaches of Kaka Point and prepare your own dinner at your crib in ⑥ Kaka Point as, apart from fish & chips, the town has no other restaurants. Before it gets dark, there is still time for a solitary walk to ⑦ Short Bay beach, which is full of driftwood on the 10-km coast road between Kaka Point and Nugget Point. There's not much nightlife here, but you can marvel at the universe under the twinkling, starry sky.

NATURE YOU COULD GET ADDICTED TO

Next day, *head south for* 🌿 ⑧ Purakaunui Bay. Here, nature is your vast cinema: the lonely bay is dominated by seals and surrounded by high cliffs and dunes. This makes swimming in the surf a real adventure. *A few minutes' drive inland,* the ⑨ Purakaunui Falls cascade 20m into the dense rainforest. You can walk to the

DAY 2
9km
⑤ Nugget Point lighthouse
9km
⑥ Kaka Point
3km
⑦ Short Bay beach

DAY 3
36km
⑧ Purakaunui Bay
11km
⑨ Purakaunui Falls

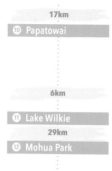

17km
⑩ Papatowai

6km
⑪ Lake Wilkie
29km
⑫ Mohua Park

waterfalls from the car park in about ten minutes. Back on the coast in ⑩ Papatowai, admire the Lost Gypsy Gallery *(Thu–Tue 10am–5pm | Papatowai Highway | thelostgypsy.com)* in a converted bus. On show are quirky artworks by Blair Somerville made from driftwood, mussels and wire. *Along the Southern Scenic Route you carry on to Tautuku.* From here, hike around the reflecting ⑪ Lake Wilkie, which is surrounded by up to 50m-tall podocarp trees. In the evening, *head back inland* to the eco-retreat ⑫ Mohua Park *(catlinsmohua park.co.nz)* in Tawanui, where you stay overnight in luxury cottages with a view over the Catlins River Valley. Before you go to sleep you should definitely try one of the Bush Walks *(approx. 20 mins)* into the rainforest on your doorstep! In the dense greenery, New Zealand is still alive as it was in the days of the first Maoris: *Wood pigeons* fly through giant ferns and between branches overgrown with moss, while above, 1,000-year-old matai trees soar upwards like giant pillars.

The lighthouse at Nugget Point has an unrivalled view of the rising sun

SAY FAREWELL BY RIDING THE WAVES

After breakfast, head for the ⑬ Cathedral Caves, 30m high rocky caves on Waipati Beach. A long path (1km) leads from the car park to the beach. The caves are only accessible at low tide! At lunchtime you can head for the ⑭ Niagara Falls Café *(daily 10am–5pm | 256 Niagara–Waikawa Road | tel. 03 246 8577 | niagarafalls cafe.co.nz | $)* in Niagara. The speciality here is smoked salmon from Stewart Island – otherwise, only local ingredients are used. The next stop is ⑮ Curio Bay. At low tide, you can see the exposed remains of a 180-million-year-old fossilized forest – the Jurassic Petrified Forest – and yellow-eyed penguins often appear. Nearby ⑯ Porpoise Bay is ideal for surfing beginners *(Catlins Surf | 4 hrs incl. board and wetsuit NZ$55 | catlinssurf.co.nz)*. If you manage to stay upright on the board and Hector's dolphins dive in the water next to you, it will be the perfect ending to your Catlins Trip!

DAY 4
37km
⑬ Cathedral Caves
26km
⑭ Niagara Falls Café
9km
⑮ Curio Bay
2km
⑯ Porpoise Bay

GOOD TO KNOW

HOLIDAY BASICS

ARRIVAL

From Europe, you can travel east or west around the globe to reach New Zealand. The flight time is about 24 hours. If you prefer, you can also turn your arrival and departure into a round-the-world trip. *Air New Zealand (airnewzealand.com)* offers flights that go via Asia and return via the US.

 + 13 hours ahead

New Zealand is 13 hours ahead of Greenwich Mean Time between the last Sunday in October and the last Sunday in March; 11 hours ahead from early April until late September; and 12 hours in between those dates.

When you book, you can decide where you want to break your journey. For example, in Singapore, L.A. or the Pacific Islands. Tip: in the airline's Premium Economy class you travel pretty much as comfortably as in Business Class. Depending on availability, at the check-in you can purchase a twin seat in the regular Economy Class, which guarantees that the seat next to you remains free (not available on all flights). If you want to stretch out during the flight, book a Skycouch in Economy Class: a seating row with three seats that transforms into a couch with folding legs; two people can recline next to each other. From 2024, Air New Zealand will even be offering bunk beds. With *Emirates (emirates.com)* you first fly to Dubai *(6½ hrs)* and from there in about 17 hours with a stopover in Australia (e.g. Sydney or Melbourne) to New Zealand. You can enjoy the airline's on-board

A stylish way to travel: cruising the streets of Napier in a vintage cabriolet

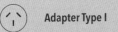

Adapter Type I

You can find an adapter for the three-pin flat plug at the airport, at petrol stations or in shops like The Warehouse.

entertainment with plenty of films and games. The journey with *Singapore Airlines (singaporeair.com)* is pleasant with a stopover in Singapore. Plenty of leg room is available with *Qatar Airways (qatarairways.com)* in the Economy Class on flights to Auckland. After a stop in Doha (often with free overnight hotel accommodation) you continue on the world's longest flight *(16½ hrs)* across ten time zones to New Zealand. In short: you can consider it a good deal if you pay between £1,000 and £1,300 for a return trip from Europe in Economy Class. You will get return trips from the US east coast for about US$1,000; from the west coast prices are significantly lower.

GETTING IN

Depending on where you come from, your passport must be valid for one or three months beyond the date you intend to depart New Zealand.

If you come from a waiver country (such as the UK) you must apply for a *New Zealand Electronic Travel Authority (NZeTA)* before you travel. You can then stay in New Zealand for up to three months. Every international visitor should pay a *levy* of approx. NZ$35 to maintain the tourist infrastructure and protect the environment. ETAs and the *levy* can be paid for together online before your arrival. Important note: for a stopover in the USA, you require an electronic passport and must apply for your ESTA authorization before you start your trip. If you are planning a stop in Asia, your passport should be valid for at least six months.

CLIMATE & WHEN TO GO

New Zealand is exposed to the vagaries of the ocean. You should be prepared – even in summer (December–February) – for sudden weather changes. You should definitely pack rainwear, a hat and down jacket (especially when you are travelling on South Island). The climate in the north of North Island is subtropical and in the south it is comparable with Central Europe. The best time to travel is during New Zealand's summer. Winter in New Zealand begins in May/June and ends in October. The skiing season on North and South Island lasts from July to September.

GETTING AROUND

BUS

If you don't have a car, you must rely on the buses. *Intercity (intercity.co.nz)* has a comprehensive network across the entire country. The route Auckland–Wellington, for example, costs about NZ$63.

For backpackers, hop-on hop-off buses are ideal, as they can be used anytime and repeatedly. *Kiwi Experience (kiwiexperience.com)* and *Stray Travel (straytravel.com)* offer reasonably priced tickets that can be used flexibly for different time intervals.

CAR

You require an international driving licence to drive on the roads in New Zealand. The traffic drives on the left, so you should look right when approaching a roundabout. Information about the most important traffic rules is at *drivesafe.org.nz*.

Journeys often take longer than expected in New Zealand because there is generally two-way traffic. You can calculate your route using the route planner on the official New Zealand website: *newzealand.com*. On highways, the maximum speed is 100kmh and in towns it's 50kmh. Mobile telephones are banned while driving. The drink-driving limit is 0.5 per mille of alcohol in the blood.

DOMESTIC FLIGHTS

Air New Zealand (airnewzealand.com) and *Jetstar (jetstar.com)* offer domestic flights in New Zealand. A flight from Auckland to Christchurch, for example, costs between NZ$120 and NZ$170.

TRAIN

Long-distance trains only travel between Auckland and Wellington *(Northern Explorer)*, Christchurch and the west coast *(TranzAlpine)* or from Picton to Christchurch *(Coastal Pacific)*. For information and booking go to: *greatjourneysofnz.co.nz*.

FERRY

Two ferries operate between North and South Island. In about three hours 30 minutes, either the *Bluebridge Ferry (bluebridge.co.nz)* or the *Interislander (greatjourneysofnz.co.nz)* takes you

FESTIVALS & EVENTS
ALL YEAR ROUND

JANUARY
Glenorchy Race Day (Lake Wakatipu): Horse races with rodeo and a folk-fest atmosphere at the north end of the lake. *glenorchyinfocentre.co.nz*

FEBRUARY
Splore (Tapapakanga Regional Park): Music festival on the coast south of Auckland. Three days to rock out in costume. With camping. *splore.net*

MARCH
Wildfoods Festival (Hokitika): A folk festival for gluttony with adventurous delicacies such as Huhu worm sushi. *wildfoods.co.nz*

APRIL
Graperide (Marlborough): Bike race with wine tasting over a 101-km beautiful, hair-raising route. *graperide.co.nz*
Bread & Circus Festival (Christchurch): Street art festival with food trucks and Ferris wheel. *breadandcircus.co.nz*

JUNE/JULY
Matariki The Maori New Year with numerous cultural events countrywide (photo). *matarikifestival.org.nz*

SEPTEMBER
World of Wearable Art (WOW) Awards Show (Wellington): Creative fashion show and design competition all in one. *worldofwearableart.com*

OCTOBER
Wellington Jazz Festival For three days, umpteen musicians descend on the capital city from all over the globe. *jazzfestival.co.nz*

DECEMBER
Rhythm & Vines (Gisborne): Multiday music festival in the vineyards. Party until the world's first sunrise of the new year. *rhythmandvines.co.nz*
Rhythm & Alps (Cardrona Valley): The sister event in the mountains in Wanaka. *rhythmandalps.co.nz*

from Wellington to Picton. You can also reach islands like Stewart Island, Waiheke or Great Barrier Island by ferry.

VEHICLE HIRE

Generally, you must be at least 21 years of age to hire a car. If you do plan to hire a vehicle: a mid-range car costs approx. NZ$80/day e.g. with *Europcar (europcar.co.nz)* or *GoRentals (go rentals.co.nz)*. You should book your camper van several months before your arrival, if possible, because demand is high, especially in summer. Also consider that a day in the camper can work out more expensive than the combination of hotel and hire car (often more than NZ$300/day). *EuroCamper (euro camper.co.nz)* and *Wendekreisen (wendekreisen.co.nz)* offer fair prices. *Share A Camper (shareacamper.com)* is a kind of Airbnb for owners of campers, who rent out their private vehicles. *Nomad Campervans (nomadnz.com)* specialises in VW camper vans. The size of camper vans ranges from smaller hi-top vans for two to three people to camper vans with six beds. When booking a camper van, you should make sure it is certified as "self-contained" (i.e. with a toilet and waste water tank). This is essential if you plan to stay overnight at the *Freedom Campsites* which are free of charge. If you cannot do without the Internet while travelling, some rental companies also offer the option to book a camper with WiFi on board.

EMERGENCIES

CONSULATES & EMBASSIES

BRITISH HIGH COMMISSION
44 Hill Street | Wellington 6011 | tel. +64 4 924 2888 | ukinnewzealand.fco. gov.uk

HIGH COMMISSION OF CANADA
Level 11, 125 The Terrace | Wellington 6011 | tel. +64 4 473 9577 | canada international.gc.ca/new_zealand-nouvelle_zelande

CONSULATE GENERAL OF THE US
3rd Floor, 23 Customs Street E | Auckland 1010 | tel. +64 4 462 6000 | nz.usembassy.gov

HEALTH
You are recommended to have the standard vaccinations before your trip. New Zealand has a very good health-care system. Tourists are entitled to free first-aid treatment in case of an accident *(accident compensation)*. Make sure you have a good travel insurance policy including repatriation in case of an emergency.

EMERGENCY CALLS

In case of an emergency, dial 111 (including from your mobile phone).

ESSENTIALS

ACCOMMODATION

You will find a wide choice of holiday houses at *bookabach.co.nz* and *holidayhouses.co.nz*. If you are travelling in a camper van or with a tent, there are several kinds of camp grounds. There are privately run campsites, which offer shared kitchens and often comfortable huts for several people *(camping pitch approx. NZ$25/person | nzcamping.com)*. About 200 camping grounds managed by the Department of Conservation (DOC) are considerably cheaper and located in remote places in the great outdoors *(from NZ$10/person)*. Facilities vary – serviced campsites with cooking bench, hot showers and toilets can be reserved with the relevant DOC Visitor Centre for the region. Campsites in the categories scenic, standard and basic generally have non-flushing toilets and a water tap with cold water and cannot be reserved in advance (they are cheaper, and occasionally free of charge). Information at *doc.govt.nz*. *Freedom Camping* grounds are free of charge throughout the country; however, these can only be used by camper vans with a toilet and wastewater tank. Information at *freedomcamping.org*. Unique cabins and glamping tents in the wilderness are offered by *Canopy Camping* *(canopycamping.co.nz)*. Backpackers can find lodgings at *yha.co.nz*, *bbh.co.nz* or *backpackerguide.nz*.

CUSTOMS

You are allowed to import e.g. 4.5 litres wine and 50 cigarettes (per person). To protect New Zealand's flora and fauna you must declare foodstuffs, plants, seeds and animal products on entry. Camping equipment and hiking boots, which are still muddy, must also be declared. If you are returning to the UK, you are permitted to carry e.g. 200 cigarettes, 4 litres spirits and gifts up to a value of £390. US residents can find information on custom regulations at *cbp.gov*.

CAUTION, BLOOD-THIRSTY MONSTERS!

Those who claim to prefer New Zealand to Australia "because there are fewer dangerous animals" haven't reckoned with the sandfly. Sandflies are mainly found on the west coast of New Zealand's South Island and in Fjordland. The catch is that they are so tiny you barely notice them, but their bites itch for days. The only protection is to wear long trousers and long-sleeved tops, even on warm days, and definitely don't save on the insect repellent! Or else only venture out when it's raining or stormy as the little pests hate bad weather.

INFORMATION

100% Pure New Zealand (newzealand. com), New Zealand's official tourism and travel website, provides information about all the country's destinations and offers plenty of tips for travel around the country.

MONEY & CREDIT CARDS

You can easily draw money with your credit card from ATMs everywhere in the country (the charges depend on the respective bank). Visa or MasterCard are accepted as a means of payment almost countrywide.

HOW MUCH DOES IT COST

Coffee	NZ$4.40
	for a take-out
Souvenirs	NZ$30
	for a pair of merino wool socks
Wine	NZ$15
	for a bottle
Bacon & egg pie	NZ$6
	for one portion
Petrol	NZ$2.70
	for one litre super
Intercity-Bus	NZ$45
	Auckland–Wellington

OPENING HOURS

Most shops are open Monday–Friday 9am–5pm and 11am–4pm at weekends. Big supermarket chains like Countdown, Pak 'n Save or New World are usually open all week until 10pm.

POST

The cost of a postcard to North America or Europe is NZ$2.80 and it takes 6–10 working days. A letter costs NZ$3.60.

PUBLIC HOLIDAYS

1 Jan	New Year
6 Feb	Waitangi Day
March/April	Good Friday/Easter Monday
25 April	ANZAC Day (Remembrance Day for servicemen and women)
1st Mon in June	King's Birthday
4th Mon in Oct	Labour Weekend
25 Dec	Christmas Day
26 Dec	Boxing Day

TELEPHONE & WIFI

The network coverage is good in all major towns and cities of the country. However, usually in the wilderness you are not just remote from world events, but also cut off from the Internet.

A "WiFi for the back pocket" can be worthwhile, when there are no public hotspots: a prepaid-SIM card from *2degrees* with 1GB of data is available for about NZ$20. With the *NZ Travel Card* from Spark for NZ$99 you get two months of up to 8GB of data, for example, plus 1GB daily, if you are in one of the country's over 1,000 *Free Spark WiFi Zones* (look out for the pink-coloured telephone boxes). The Internet is now available free of charge in most accommodation, in libraries and most i-Sites (visitor information), and in plenty of cafés. A map of the country with all free WiFi hotspots is available at *wifispc. com*.

There are four mobile phone providers in New Zealand: *Vodafone (vodafone.co.nz)*, *2Degrees (2degrees mobile.co.nz)*, *Spark (spark.co.nz)* and *Skinny (skinny.co.nz)*. All are available e.g. at The Warehouse, where you can buy a SIM card of the relevant provider, which will allow you to make cheap calls within New Zealand.

The country code for New Zealand is 0064. When making a call from New Zealand, dial 0044 for the United Kingdom; 001 for the US and Canada; and 0061 for Australia.

TIPPING

In New Zealand it is not usual to leave a tip. When you leave a restaurant you normally pay at the bar.

Historic letter box in Auckland

WEATHER IN WELLINGON

High season
Low season

	JAN	FEB	MARCH	APRIL	MAY	JUNE	JULY	AUG	SEPT	OCT	NOV	DEC
Daytime temperature	21°	21°	19°	17°	14°	13°	12°	12°	14°	16°	17°	19°
Night-time temperature	13°	13°	12°	11°	8°	7°	6°	6°	8°	9°	10°	12°
Hours of sunshine per day	8	7	6	5	4	4	4	4	6	6	7	7
Rainy days per month	7	4	5	10	11	14	14	15	10	10	11	10
Sea temperature in °C	17°	18°	18°	17°	14°	14°	13°	13°	12°	14°	14°	17°

☀ Hours of sunshine per day   🌧 Rainy days per month   ≈ Sea temperature in °C

Steampunk Festival, Waikato

HOLIDAY VIBES

FOR RELAXATION & CHILLING

FOR BOOKWORMS & FILM BUFFS

🎥 THE POWER OF THE DOG

This visually stunning drama from director Jane Campion tells the story of two very different brothers. The film won the 2022 Academy Award for Best Director and was filmed across New Zealand, including in Dunedin and the Maniototo region in Central Otago.

📖 THE LUMINARIES

The novel (2013) by Booker Prize-winner Eleanor Catton is set during the gold rush in Hokitika in the wild west of South Island. Perfect reading for the long flight to New Zealand

🎥 HUNT FOR THE WILDERPEOPLE

Adventure comedy (2016) about the orphan kid Ricky by New Zealand cult director Taika Waititi *(JoJo Rabbit, Thor)* with magical shots of the scenery and typical Kiwi humour.

📖 NOTHING VENTURE, NOTHING WIN

Beekeeper turned mountaineer: in his autobiography, Sir Edmund Hillary, born in Auckland in 1919, tells of his hikes on Mount Cook, expeditions to the South Pole and, of course, his famous first ascent of Mount Everest.

PLAYLIST
THE KIWI SOUND

`0:58`

II LORDE – ROYALS
Global favourite and award-winning song of the year at the 2014 Grammys.

▶ ALDOUS HARDING – THE BARREL
Chilled indie folk tune, the perfect road trip anthem for a journey through New Zealand.

▶ BENEE – SUPALONELY
The then 20-year-old pop singer's lockdown hit took the global charts by storm back in 2020.

▶ THE CHILLS – PINK FROST
Indie song from the 1980s that helped shaped that special Dunedin sound.

▶ CROWDED HOUSE – DON'T DREAM IT'S OVER
Sung by New Zealander Neil Finn, this is one of the most famous pop ballads of the eighties.

The holiday soundtrack is available on **Spotify** under **MARCO POLO** New Zealand

Or scan this code with the Spotify app

ONLINE

BREADCRUMBS
Top tips for surfing spots, hidden waterfalls and craft beer bars: users recommend their favourite places on the app. That's how you discover places you'd otherwise never find.

CAMPER MATE
Super handy app with an offline map that shows all campsites nationwide. Info on prices, toilet and shower facilities and sewage disposal is regularly updated. Pitches can also be booked

UNDER THE RADAR
The best resource to learn about New Zealand's music scene and gigs big and small (undertheradar.co.nz).

GRAB ONE
Cheap deals for outdoor activities, restaurants, hotels and spa treatments (grabone.co.nz).

JELLY JOURNEYS
Two travel vloggers from England share their outdoor adventures; river

TRAVEL PURSUIT

THE MARCO POLO HOLIDAY QUIZ

Do you know your facts about New Zealand? Here you can test your knowledge of the little secrets and idiosyncrasies of the country and its people. You will find the correct answers below, with further details on pages 22 to 27 of this guide.

❶ What are the All Blacks rugby team famous for always doing?
a) They sing the national anthem in Maori
b) Every player must weigh at least 100 kg
c) They perform a warrior dance before every match

❷ What *doesn't* the word kiwi apply to?
a) A cactus
b) A New Zealander
c) A bird

❸ New Zealand is called Aotearoa in Maori. What does that mean?
a) Land of the wind
b) Land of the long white cloud
c) Land of the ferns

❹ How much can you be fined for wild camping if you don't have a chemical toilet with you?
a) NZ$500
b) NZ$1,000
c) NZ$700

❺ What is the Maori nose kiss called?
a) Hangi
b) Hungi
c) Hongi

Answers: 1c, 2a, 3b, 4b, 5c, 6c, 7b, 8a, 9b, 10c, 11c, 12b

What do you call a kiwi doing winter sports?

❻ Which creatures did not exist in New Zealand before people populated the land?
a) Birds
b) Lizards
c) Predators

❼ How long have there been tuataras in New Zealand?
a) 2.5 million years
b) 225 million years
c) 25 million years

❽ How many bungy jumps did world record-holder Mike Heard complete in 24 hours?
a) 430
b) 280
c) 170

❾ What was Sir Edmund Hillary's job before climbing Mount Everest?
a) Sheep shearer
b) Beekeeper
c) Cattle farmer

❿ What is New Zealand's national plant?
a) Pohutukawa
b) Kauri
c) Silver fern

⓫ What is Auckland's nickname?
a) City of volcanoes
b) City between the oceans
c) City of sails

⓬ Which city hosts people dressed up in 1920s style?
a) Rotorua
b) Napier
c) Oamaru

INDEX

WE WANT TO HEAR FROM YOU!

Did you have a great holiday? Is there something on your mind? Whatever it is, let us know! Whether you want to praise the guide, alert us to errors or give us a personal tip – MARCO POLO would be pleased to hear from you. Please contact us by email:

We do everything we can to provide the very latest information for your trip. Nevertheless, despite all of our authors' thorough research, errors can creep in. MARCO POLO does not accept any liability for this.

sales@heartwoodpublishing.co.uk

PICTURE CREDITS
Cover photo: Otago, Otago Peninsula, View from Sandymount Recreation Reserve to Allans Beach (huber-images: R. Mirau)

Photos: DuMont Bildarchiv: Emmler (129), Schröder/Schwarzbach (39, 96, 117); Getty Images/EyeEm: B. Lucka (32); Getty Imahes: O. Strewe (74); huber-images: M. Breitung (23, 72, 77), J. Foulkes (2/3, 70), M. Rellini (162/163), M. Ripani (140/141), M. Simoni (63), F. Tremolada (28/29); laif: Emmler (34/35, 36/37, 82, 123), Hauser (8/9), Knop (126); laif/Le Figaro Magazine: Fautre (back cover flap, 86/87), Martin (30/31); Look: K. Johaentges (152/153), B. van Dierendonck (78); Look/age fotostock (132/133); Look/Axiom (105); Look/Minden Pictures (108); Look/robertharding (91); mauritius images: F. Berlich (69), W. Bibikow (35), R. Mirau (134/135), M. Schindler (130); mauritius images/AA World Travel Library/Alamy (127); mauritius images/age: B. Harrington (52); mauritius images/Alamy (10, T. Cuff (139), G. B. Evans (16/17), B. Harrington III (24), R. Piccioli (13), P. Quayle (55), T. Uhlman (84), K. Vlessis (120); mauritius images/Alamy/Alamy Photo Stock: R. Mogado (102); mauritius images/Alamy/Alamy Stock Photos: R. Armstrong (57), B. Christian (66), I. Dagnall (115), P. Dudek (14/15), B. Scantlebury (144), D. Wall (12, 31); mauritius images/Alamy/Alamy Stock Photos/Danita Delimont Creative (inside and outside cover flaps); mauritius images/Alamy/Alamy Stock Photos/Stockimo: L. Grieveson (155); mauritius images/Alamy/Alamy Stock Photos/Visions from Earth (64); mauritius images/Danita Delimont (107, R. Bishop (101); mauritius images/imagebroker: M. Rucker (26/27), M. Wolf (10, 150); mauritius images/Minden Pictures/Colin Monteath/Hedgehog-House (124/125); mauritius images/MJ Photography/Alamy (11); mauritius images/Nature in Stock: B. Ooms (92); mauritius images/nature picture library: B. Stephenson (113); mauritius images/Pitopia/PRILL Mediendesign & Fotografie (118); mauritius images/robertharding: N. Clark (42/43), M. Williams-Ellis (47, 49, 59); mauritius images/TPG RF (98); mauritius images/Westend61: J.&N. Boerner (60), H. Spiering (21), G. Wojciech (164/165); A. Tiedemann (167); Shutterstock.com: BrianScantlebury (6/7), Emagnetic (159), Valentine Gladysheff (160/161).

4th Edition – fully revised and updated 2023
Worldwide Distribution: Heartwood Publishing Ltd, Bath, United Kingdom
www.heartwoodpublishing.co.uk

Authors: Katja May, Aileen Tiedemann
Editor: Christina Sothmann
Picture editor: Gabriele Forst
Cartography: © MAIRDUMONT, Ostfildern (pp. 40–41, 136, 145, 147, 149, outside jacket, pull-out map); © MAIRDUMONT, Ostfildern, using data from OpenStreetMap, licence CC-BY-SA 2.0 (pp.44–45, 51, 81, 88–89, 94, 100)
Cover design and pull-out map cover design: bilekjaeger_Kreativagentur with Zukunftswerkstatt, Stuttgart
Page design: Langenstein Communication GmbH, Ludwigsburg

Heartwood Publishing credits:
Translated from the German by Madeleine Taylor-Laidler and Dr Suzanne Kirkbright
Editors: Felicity Laughton, Kate Michell, Sophie Blacksell Jones
Prepress: Summerlane Books, Bath
Printed in India

MARCO POLO AUTHOR
AILEEN TIEDEMANN

Aileen Tiedemann is a freelance travel writer for magazines and news sites. New Zealand is particularly close to her heart as her partner is a Kiwi. The couple make sure they travel to the country regularly with their daughter; they start getting itchy feet as soon as they see the All Blacks perform the *Haka*, the Maori war dance, before a rugby match in Hamburg, Germany!